A LIFE IN
CONVERSATION

Books by Bernard J. Lee, S.M.

The Becoming of the Church
Religious Experience and Process Theology (with Harry James Cargas)
Alternative Futures for Worship (General Editor)
Dangerous Memories (with Michael Cowan)
The Galileean Jewishness of Jesus
Jesus and the Metaphors of God
The Future Church of 140 BCE
Conversation, Risk & Conversion (with Michael Cowan)
Habits for the Journey
The Catholic Experience of Small Christian Communities
Gathered and Sent (with Michael Cowan)
The Beating of Great Wings
The Re- Becoming of the Church

A LIFE IN CONVERSATION

Essays in Honor of Bernard J. Lee, S.M.

WRITTEN BY HIS COLLEAGUES
and FORMER STUDENTS
MICHAEL A. COWAN, EDITOR

TRUE DIRECTIONS
AN AFFILIATE OF TARCHER BOOKS

iUniverse®

A LIFE IN CONVERSATION
ESSAYS IN HONOR OF BERNARD J. LEE, S.M.

Michael A. Cowan, Editor

iUniverse books may be ordered through booksellers or by contacting:

iUniverse
1663 Liberty Drive
Bloomington, IN 47403
www.iuniverse.com
1-800-Authors (1-800-288-4677)

ISBN: 978-1-4917-6281-3 (sc)
ISBN: 978-1-4917-6280-6 (hc)
ISBN: 978-1-4917-6279-0 (e)

Library of Congress Control Number: 2015903884

Print information available on the last page.

iUniverse rev. date: 04/30/2015

Contents

Contributors

Dianne Bergant, C.S.A.
Catholic Theological Union, Chicago
Michael A. Cowan
Institute for Ministry, Loyola University New Orleans
Nancy Dallavalle
Religious Studies and University Mission and Identity, Fairfield University
William V. D'Antonio
Institute for Policy Research and Catholic Studies, Catholic University
Peter J. Eichten
Metropolitan State University, St. Paul; St. Frances Cabrini Catholic Church, Minneapolis
Thomas F. Giardino, S.M.
Association of Marianist Universities
Bernard J. Lee, S.M.
Department of Theology, St. Mary's University, San Antonio
Andrew Simon Sleeman, O.S.B.
Glenstal Abbey, Ireland
Terry A. Veling
Faculty of Philosophy and Theology, Australian Catholic University
Evelyn and James Whitehead
Institute of Pastoral Studies, Loyola University Chicago

Acknowledgments

In 2011, Professor Terry Veling, a contributor to this volume, proposed the creation of a volume of essays to honor Professor Bernard J. Lee, S.M. on the occasion of his 80th birthday. The essays were presented in a meeting at St. Mary's University in San Antonio on Bernard's birthday, July 14, 2012. This volume makes those essays available to the public.

The contributors wish to thank Fr. Rudy Vela, S.M., and Ms. Cindy Stooksberry of St. Mary's Office of Mission for organization and warm hospitality, and the Society of Mary for financial support for the gathering. We acknowledge a generous anonymous donation as well.

Michael A. Cowan

Dedication

To my Marianist confreres
Who conjoin
The love of scholarship
With the love of community

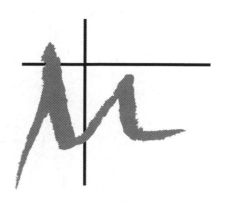

By size I mean the stature of a person's soul, the range and depth of your love, your capacity for relationships. I mean the volume of life you can take into your being and still maintain your integrity and individuality, the intensity and variety of outlooks you can entertain. I mean the strength of your spirit to encourage others to become freer in the development of their diversity and uniqueness. I mean the power to sustain more complex and enriching tensions. I mean the magnanimity of concern to provide conditions that enable others to increase in stature.

Bernard J. Loomer

Introduction

A Life in Conversation

Michael A. Cowan

A genuine conversation is never the one that we wanted to conduct.

Hans-Georg Gadamer

When I was a newly minted Ph.D. and university faculty member, two colleagues of mine, one a political scientist and the other a theologian and economist, decided that our small liberal arts college in the woods of central Minnesota needed a dialogue between social science and theology. Being too young in the academy to have learned that what passes for dialogue there, as in the rest of the world, often involves talking without listening, debate without mutual understanding, and politics with little at stake beyond individual or departmental perks, I showed up. The three years of group conversation that ensued set me on a path that I have never left, but rather continues to lead me in surprising directions.

Group meetings that took place without transcripts thirty years ago are remembered selectively and perhaps apocryphally as well. My personal recall of the "Social Science-Theology Dialogue" at St. John's University (Collegeville) goes like this. The fifteen participating theologians and social scientists agreed that one of us would prepare a brief paper to be the focus for each month's dialogue. The papers were distributed and read in advance. At the beginning of each meeting, the author would make a few comments and open the floor for questions and reactions. In the initial sessions we took turns, allowing each presenter to have their say, followed by questions and statements of agreement or disagreement.

Then, after a few pleasant but unremarkable meetings, something happened that sent our dialogue in a direction that I came to regard as the birth of my intellectual life. One member suggested that instead of just taking turns politely listening to one another, we stop the presenter when he or she said something that just didn't make sense from our point of view and ask them to explain the statement from their disciplinary perspective, to help us understand how they saw something in the world in that way. We would speak to explain and listen to understand. Not refute, not debate, not try to make points, but attempt to explain and comprehend the world from the vantage points of a sacramental theologian, an economist and expert in theological ethics, a "process" philosopher/theologian, a political scientist, a church historian, a linguistic philosopher, a sociologist and others. As a young psychologist with interests in psychotherapy, group communication, and adult development, I felt my horizon of understanding cracking open. I still remember the moment 40 years ago when it dawned on me that when I said the word "personality," my sociologist colleague wasn't envisioning habitual intrapsychic states, but rather patterns of relating within a structured social world—roles, statuses and styles.

The human mind, or at least my human mind, needs to locate new learning within some larger context of understanding. My discipline of origin, psychology, could no longer hold what I was learning to see. In the immediately succeeding years, I became for the first time a student in the true sense, seeking the truth wherever it led me, immersing myself especially in philosophy, theology and sociology. After a long time of creative disorientation, I eventually found my larger framework in philosophy, in the understandings of person, society and history that underlie every discipline. I ended up back in graduate school. I departed from a long-planned career path, and changed my vocational course again ten years later. And I have never strayed from the path the group illuminated for me. Its name is "conversation."

The "someone" who changed the trajectory of our group—and my life with it—was Bernard Lee.

The life in conversation of the authors of this volume, and many others, with Bernard Lee is like Mary, full of grace. Some fruits of those dialogues may be sampled between these covers, and this is only a taste of the relational harvest for which Bernard is responsible. With these essays we thank and salute our honored colleague and friend, looking forward to the futures of the conversations he continues to inspire and their descendants.

Chapter 1

Maintaining Our Astonishment

A Reflection on Key Teachings from Bernard J. Lee, S.M.

Terry A. Veling

Introduction

> Shortly before his death, Rabbi Nahman, the great grandson of the Baal Shem Tov, spoke to his disciples. "Why come to me? I do not know anything." He repeated several times, sincerely, that he did not know anything. Then he began to speak and to teach. "It is forbidden to grow old," he said. "It is necessary to start over, each time." "One must maintain one's astonishment."

In various conversations with Bernard, I have heard him say in his inimitable style, "finitude sucks." Perhaps Rabbi Nahman would agree: "It is forbidden to grow old." Whether we are eight or eighty, it remains "necessary to start over, each time," and to "maintain one's astonishment." One of the delights of knowing Bernard and interacting with his work is that while he is always attentive to the concrete realities and givens of life, he is also mindful that "something else might be the case" (GJ, 1). Indeed, back in the seventies, Bernard was already saying, "the movement of history is a *creative advance*" (RE, 372). We are not merely beings-toward-death, we are beings-toward-life. It is not decay and growing old that marks our life, but the ever-present possibility of new beginnings, creative advances, and "alternative futures" (to use the title from Bernard's series on worship). It is this commitment to life, and to the God of life, that enables us, along with Bernard, to "maintain our astonishment."

This essay is structured around six key teachings I have learned from Bernard (among others), encapsulated in sayings such as, "it matters" or "presence is what takes hold of me" or "the person of size." Along with excerpts from Bernard's own writings, I have interwoven some of the authors who are significant to Bernard and, through him, also significant to me. Many of Bernard's teachings have stayed with me for a long time. I often find myself passing them on to my own students, such that "generations" are now involved in Bernard's life. As the great Talmudic sage Rashi comments: "When one teaches the Torah to the sons and daughters of our fellow human beings, it is as if one had engendered them oneself. The true descendants are students, those whom one has taught."[1] Bernard's generative influence is indeed "generational."

1. It matters

"It matters. It has consequences."

Bernard has sometimes wished he could take credit for these words, but they come from Alfred North Whitehead, though I suspect they would be lost to history if it were not for Bernard's constant retelling. The story, as Bernard relays it, goes like this. One of Whitehead's students came up to him after class and asked, "Professor Whitehead, how would you characterize reality?" Whitehead put down his books, remaining silent for a few minutes, then replied, "It matters. It has consequences."

This saying appears very early in Bernard's work. In a chapter titled, "The Appetite for God," he writes: "We matter deeply to and in the actuality of God. There is no way not to have a hankering . . . for that which matters deeply" (RE, 373). And then, in his dedication to *The Future Church of 140 BCE*, Bernard writes: "Most of the things/that today I believe/matter most/and have consequences/that are full of grace.

Reality counts. Things matter. Life requires us. And even though we are only here "once" – or maybe because we are only here once – our lives on earth are heavy with consequences that can never be cancelled. "Whatever you bind on earth will be bound in heaven, and whatever you loose on earth will be released in heaven" (*Matthew* 18:18 NRSV).[2] The deeds we perform may seem slight, yet they carry consequences that affect the lives of those around us, and maybe even the lives of those distant to us. According to Rabbi Hayyim Volozhiner: "Let nobody in Israel – God forbid! – ask himself: 'What am I, and what can my humble acts achieve in the world?' Let him rather understand this, that he may know it and fix it in his thoughts: not one detail of his acts, of his words and of his thoughts, is ever lost."[3]

Our actions and words are not performed or spoken into a vacuum or a void. They can do good or harm; they can bind or release; they bear responsibility; they carry the weight of life and death, of good and evil. Abraham Heschel perhaps captures this best when he writes: "Significant living is an attempt to adjust to what is expected and required of being human. This sense of requiredness is as essential to being human as the capacity for reasoning... This sense of requiredness is not an afterthought; it is given with being human, not added to it but rooted in it."[4]

According to Bernard, "the really rare question is: What kind of world do we want to make for ourselves and our children?" (FC, 116; BGW, 151). It is interesting that Bernard calls this a "rare question." Perhaps we aren't asking it often enough; perhaps we aren't addressing it often enough. Perhaps this is the question that really matters.

2. The Person of Size

On many occasions I have heard Bernard refer to "the person of size." This phrase comes from Bernard's early encounter with process philosopher, Bernard Loomer. In at least two of his texts, Bernard includes substantial excerpts from Loomer's work, having to do with "relational power" and "the person of size." In terms of the latter, Loomer writes:

> By *size* I mean the stature of a person's soul, the range and depth of his love, his capacity for relationships. I mean the volume of life you can take into your being . . . the intensity and variety of outlooks you can entertain . . . I

mean the strength of your spirit to encourage others to
become freer in the development of their diversity and
uniqueness. I mean the power to sustain more complex
and enriching tensions. I mean the magnanimity of
concern to provide conditions that enable others to
increase in stature.[5]

This passage evokes the very spirit of Bernard's life and work:
capacity for relationships, depth of love, openness to ever-new learning,
encouraging others in their own diversity and uniqueness, largeness of
spirit, and enabling others to increase in dignity and stature.

Another word that Bernard evokes that also expresses this spirit. It is
the French word, from Gabriel Marcel, *disponibilité*. It is usually translated
as "availability," though as Bernard suggests, it is "more like sitting on
the edge of your chair, leaning forward out of readiness and eagerness to
be met" (BGW, 144; RE, 378). Marcel says it is "being ready to receive,"
"making room for the other in myself."[6] (88). It is the act of dedicating
oneself to the other. Marcel links disposability ("being at your disposal")
with creativity – I give myself to the person or to the production of some
work, not for the sake of one's small ego, but for the sake of the enlargement
of life and participation in God's creative goodness. Bernard, of course, is a
Marianist, and perhaps one of the classic examples of *disponibilité* is Mary's
response to the angel's annunciation: "Here I am, the servant of the Lord,
let it be with me according to your word" (*Luke* 1:38). Mary said "yes" at the
very beginning, making room for the other in herself; she "formed Christ
in her womb and labored to bring him forth into the world" (HJ, xiii).

According to Bernard, a person of size and *disponibilité* is formed
in the ongoing requirement and engagement of conversation. In various
texts he outlines a process or a model for conversation (FC, 124-136).
This process is about "making friends" with each other – enhancing
relationships and making meanings and new worlds together – and it is
also about "making friends with our sacred texts" (AF, 157-173). It is a
process of receptivity ("availability") and enlargement (becoming people
of "size"). Here is what Bernard says about the essence of conversation:

I cannot listen seriously to a different life and come away
unchanged . . . I risk being required to alter my sense of

things, my understandings, my values, my *self*... I am not only reconstructing and re-understanding the meaning of my friend (or my sacred text), I am reconstructing the meaning of myself.

Relationship means co-creation of each other's identity. When there is co-creation, no one person has control. Thus a relationship always opens up new possibilities for both lives. The conversation of a relationship makes new things appear out in front of both participants. Something is made by the conversation: a possible world is conjured up and projected; a story gets a new plot or possibility; history is enriched by a new version of how it might be lived. (AF, 160-61)

We become people of size when we risk our pre-conceived worlds, when we open ourselves to new possibilities, when we co-create each other, when we work together for a "new version" of personal and communal life.

3. Presence

The concept of "presence," if it can be called a concept, appears early in Bernard's work. "Whatever shapes or creates me in any way is present to and in me. Presence refers to whatever has a hold on my becoming" (RE, 286). And then in *The Future Church of 140BCE*: "Presence does not primarily mean here rather than there, today rather than yesterday, close rather than far. It has more to do with whomever and whatever has played a large constitutive role in my experience" (FC, 61).

We can live our lives unattentively, unthinkingly, routinely – and presence will always elude us. Or we can allow things to touch us, to take hold of our becoming, to stir our souls, to enter our world. By "things" I do not mean "objects" – rather, I mean the "thou-like" quality of the people and events of our lives, the sacred texts and symbols of our tradition, the questions and concerns of our age.

Presence infuses everything with life and vitality. There is no need to posit a divine world; the world is already naturally divine. "There is no thing in the world in which there is not life," a Hasidic master says, "and each has the form of life in which it stands before your eyes. And lo, this life is the life of God."[7]

There is a holy spark in every living creature and every human being. Presence presumes energy and life, rather than an indifferent or anonymous existence. Presence means that things are diaphanous and alive, such that each living being blazes with intense singularity and uniqueness. Presence is a marvel and a miracle, and super, super natural. Presence requires an alert receptivity, a keen reflective attentiveness that, in the words of David Tracy,

> embarks upon a journey of intensification into the concreteness of each particular reality – *this* body, *this* people, *this* community, *this* tradition, *this* tree, *this* place, this *moment, this* neighbor – until the very concreteness in any particularity releases us to sense the concreteness of the whole as internally related through and through.[8]

Inherent in Bernard's writings is the conviction that there should be no separation between the love of God and the love of neighbor. Perhaps there is nothing worse than a spirituality that cannot accommodate humanity. It is, rather, our spiritual duty to become human. This "becoming human" is not a task we set ourselves to achieve; rather, it is a task given us by divine life. If the task of religious faith is to try to "humanize" our world, or to "personalize" our world, or to overcome the world of "It" and welcome the presence of "Thou," then surely this is also what it means to "divinize" our world.

Presence in life presumes communication and the very real possibility of dialogue, if only we could listen and be attentive, if only we could believe that there are, as George Steiner reminds us, "real presences" in life, real signs of vitality and personality. Bernard cites Heschel: "There are no proofs for the existence of the God of Abraham. There are only witnesses." He goes on to say: "Experience cannot prove God. The experience of God is not about proving. It is about testifying" (FC, 56).

It is rare to encounter a text by Bernard without the inclusion, somewhere along the way, of poetry and even artwork. Presence is closely aligned with the aesthetic – which enlivens us with beauty and grace – rather than the anaesthetic, which dulls our senses and deadens our soul. The artistic work, says Steiner, comes to us as a visitation and a summons – "an Annunciation of a terrible beauty or gravity breaking into the small house of our cautionary being. If we have heard rightly the wing-beat and provocation of that visit, our house is no longer habitable in quite the same way as before."[9] One of Bernard's most recent books is titled, *The Beating of Great Wings*. In the epigraph to this text, Bernard cites a poetic text from Henry Nelson Wieman, noting that the annunciation and the visitation always requires some measure of dying and brokenness: "We must be broken because there is a good so great it breaks the bounds of our littleness."

Life is full of joyous, sorrowful and glorious mysteries. "If we listen together very quietly, I wager we can hear, albeit ever so faintly, the beating of great wings" (BGW, 2). Maybe these great wings are like the Spirit hovering over creation. When we become aware of Presence, it is almost impossible for our hearts not to be stirred by response. Rabbi Lawrence Kushner captures this in his *Book of Words*: "You become aware that you are in the Presence. What then? Silence? Song? Blessing? Candles? Charity? Study? Reaching out to another? Just these are the beginning of the response."[10]

Presence is perhaps another word for what the Catholic tradition calls "sacramentality." Sacramentality means that what we perceive as ordinary (it's only or merely this) suddenly becomes extraordinary (it's actually or really this!). The things of our lives often mean so much more when we infuse them with a sacramental sense of "real presence." For example, a table with lit candles, bread, and a carafe of wine stands in readiness for the guests to arrive. Many of us know Bernard's love of cooking and offering hospitality. The sharing of a meal and wine reminds us that human beings always seem to discover a sense of communion when they eat and drink together. Bernard writes: "Presence happens when God exercises a hold on our becoming, when God makes a difference, when the Christ-event clarifies God's intentions in specific events, when the Spirit creates in us an appetite for God" (BGW, 38).

4. Attend to life – this is the best way to attend to God

When I was a young graduate student, one of the first books Bernard handed me to read was Hans-Georg Gadamer's *Truth and Method*, a brick-like tome of some 600 pages![11] A "book of size," indeed, with equally sizeable insights. I learnt almost all I know about hermeneutics from Bernard's engagement with thinkers such as Gadamer. One of the many insights that have remained with me is that the art of interpretation is intimately tied to the art of creativity, and this is as it should be, for the *creativity of a work* necessarily calls forth the *creativity of the interpreter.* This active engagement with sacred texts and great works of literature and art is indelibly inscribed in Bernard's own writings.

Bernard once complimented my own work by saying it is "thorough and in the mood of Gabriel Marcel, systematically unsystematic!"[12] If this is what endeared my work to Bernard, it can only be because I was inspired by his own "systematically unsystematic" approach. Yet, what does "systematically unsystematic" mean? It is like a Zen koan. Perhaps it means ensuring that our approaches to life, sacred texts and each other are taken seriously, yet as shot-through with existential concern – given in life and not detached in theoretical remoteness. "All systems of thought sooner or later exhaust their ability to illuminate experience" (JM, 184). In his "autobiographical tracings," Bernard notes the importance of Marcel. "I most appreciated Marcel's reminder that experience itself is not perfectly orderly and angular, but often random and meandering." He goes on to say, "I took all the orderly outlines that I had prepared for my high school religion classes and burned them, and resolved to let each class evolve anew ever after" (GJ, 10).

It would be impossible to read Bernard's work without noticing his unwavering commitment to "radical empiricism" and the immediacies of "concrete experience." "The worldly presences of God are the data of theology," he writes. "Religious empiricism can be stated that simply" (BGW, 32). Or again: "God is available to us in every drop of experience" (FC, 59-60). Or yet again: "Events are laden. They are heavy with a thousand causes. They are luminous with a thousand references. They laugh or cry with a thousand feelings" (BGW, 27).

Bernard is not speaking simply or solely of "sense experience" (though he does not discount this), nor is he denying the importance of the intellectual life. However, he suggests that our use of reason and systematic thought often functions like a thin layer of oil that is floating on a deeper body of water. Paul Ricoeur, for example, suggests that it is the realm of the poetic and the symbolic that "gives rise to thought."[13] Similarly, Bernard notes that the production of concepts and ideas, which often appear to us as clear and distinct, are like thin abstractions of meaning that float on a vaster reserve of poetic and intuitive life. Religious perception, rather than being vague or indistinct, is often more in touch with the depth of human experience than the generalized abstractions of rational consciousness. "Vague and shadowy experience is not less real because of its indistinctness, but fuller, richer, more immediate and more complete." (GJ, 28) Systematically derived thought is often quite abstract, whereas "concreteness lies with the vague, not with the clear!" (GJ, 30). Our rational ways of knowing have tended to neglect deeper, intuitive ways of knowing, or what Bernard Meland calls an "appreciative consciousness"[14] We live more deeply than we think. If we are to be faithful to lived experience, this "more deeply" needs to be reflected in our ways of knowing.

Bernard also notes the influence of Teilhard de Chardin. "*The Divine Milieu* assured me of the holiness of the world, the holiness of matter, and the availability of the living God in my direct experience of the world" (GJ, 11). Bernard embraces both a love for God and a healthy love for the world: "I have never wanted to ignore the world to be with God. My family gave me ground-loving feet. And Teilhard gave me a ground-loving God." (GJ, 11)

Attention to life in the world and to human experience is therefore crucial. As Bernard notes: "When 'something about' human experience is also in some genuine way 'something about God,' we can use that element of human experience to put us in touch with the something about God" (RE, 378-79).

Bernard also acknowledges the gift of the American pragmatic tradition. We should never leave ideas to the realm of abstraction; rather, ideas are only worth their salt if they are "put to work" or tested in concrete situations. "If you want to know what an idea means," Bernard writes, "see what it does, what habits of action it produces." To learn what something means, "we must put it to work in the stream of experience" (BGW, 49).

Bernard is a poetic as well as a practical soul. He often cites Johann-Baptist Metz's claim that Christians must be both mystical and prophetic. He offers the following quote from Metz in the epigraph to *Habits for the Journey*:

> Following Christ is always a twofold structure ... mystical and political at one and the same time. When the double mystical and political composition of following Christ is

ignored, what happens is either the reduction of following Christ to a purely social and political dimension of behaviour or its reduction to private religious spirituality.

Lastly, Bernard's work is marked by a constant effort to reclaim Hebrew patterns of thinking and acting in contrast to the predominance of a Greek-styled philosophy of speculative reason. God is not the distant, unaffected, "unmoved mover." Rather, God is very much the "moved mover" who participates in the world's travails (GJ, 81, 133). Heschel describes this as "prophetic pathos" – "feeling with" rather than remaining distant and aloof or, even worse, indifferent. "The basic feature of pathos," Heschel writes, "is *divine attentiveness and concern* . . . a divine attentiveness to humanity, an involvement in history, a divine vision of the world . . . This is the most precious insight: to sense God's participation in existence, to experience oneself as a divine secret."[15] Similarly, Bernard writes: "The future is God's secret and God's promise, and it is in the present that we open ourselves to new prospects for God's intentions for the world." (BGW, 5)

I am reminded of two sayings from the Rabbinic tradition, brought to my attention by Heschel's masterful study, *Heavenly Torah*.[16] The first saying states that the Torah "is not in heaven" (cf. *Deuteronomy* 30:12). Rather, it is given to us – "on earth" – to wrestle with its teachings and to activate its meanings. Interpretation always means that I am implicated, that the text is speaking to me, to this community, here and now, today. I am required. The second saying states that the "Torah is a gift from heaven." It communicates or reveals God's intentions for the world; it guides us along the path of life; it teaches us how to live "on earth, as it is in heaven." It seems to me that much of Bernard's work is indeed "all earthly and all heavenly." In Christian language, one might be tempted to say that the incarnate word also expresses or reveals the transcendent word. The finite also "contains" or reveals the infinite. Thus the finite is to be treasured as the honored place where the infinite comes to pass. The Christian tradition wagers that there is an intimate relationship between human experience – living, suffering, joyous – and the word of God – born, crucified, risen. We always live with the possibility of hearing and responding to "the Word become flesh." Bernard writes: "One doesn't lead a Christian life through having heard the Word just once. It is the constant effective contact of the Word with our living that increases the density of God's presence to us" (BGW, 38).

5. Word and World

Bernard exclaims: "What we can know, whether intuitionally or perceptually or conceptually, must originate in what is given to us in relationship. Period!" (GJ, 30). Whether our engagement is with each other (personally or communally), or with our sacred texts, or with the poetic or symbolic world, or with the beauty of the natural world – all this is given to us in relationship. "Period!"

This relational quality is perhaps best encapsulated when Bernard speaks of the ongoing and always potentially creative conversation between "Word and world" (BGW, 6). "When I say *the Word*," Bernard writes, "I mean it as a symbol for the storehouse of Christian riches, as well as more specifically the Scriptures. These are all voices of faith which deserve to be brought into conversation with the world in which we live – the faith of Abraham and Sarah, Moses and Miriam, Mary, Elizabeth, Peter, Paul, Augustine, Aquinas, Catherine of Siena, Teresa, John of the Cross, William Joseph Chaminade . . ." (HJ, 26). It is this "dialogue between the word and the world that clarifies God's intentions and how they should be implemented" (BGW, 47). And again: "The seriousness with which we take earth *now* is a commitment to do something significant, *now, here.* To be a history maker. To be a world maker. To be a dream maker. To be a kingdom maker on earth as it is in heaven" (FC, 104-05).

Bernard is prompting us toward a "Godly world" and a "worldly God" (BGW, 83). This is akin to the Catholic sacramental tradition. The world is a sacrament of God (*sacramentum mundi*), mediating our experience of God (BGW, 88). Bernard writes: "All of life – like all of the world – has the possibility of mediating the transformative encounter between God and human history. That is its sacramental character" (AF, 9). And again: "It is when the events in which we are engaged call us to decision that the personal speech of God occurs" (BGW, 7).

As noted earlier, Bernard is keen to evoke Hebrew sensibilities. He does this especially by reclaiming the Hebrew word, "*dabar.*" This is difficult to translate; Bernard suggests "deedword" (BGW, 42). In Hebrew,

God's word is active, creative, continually bringing forth life and existence. One of the names attributed to God by the rabbinic sages is "the One who spoke and the world came into being." The prophet Isaiah puts it this way: "As the rain and the snow come down from heaven, and do not return until they have watered the earth, making it bring forth and sprout . . . so shall my word be that goes forth from my mouth; it shall not return to me empty, but it shall accomplish that which I purpose . . ." (55: 10-11). We too can share in this creative word of God. We are in the world to love and name the world, to create, to bring forth life. As Bernard so often notes, we are historical actors more than we are contemplative spectators. (BGW, 98-101; FC, 106-08). Teilhard de Chardin perhaps captures this sense when he speaks of the "divinization of our activities." He writes: "In action I adhere to the creative power of God; I coincide with it; I become not only its instrument but its living extension."[17]

Bernard never ceases to re-energize the discipline that is called, for want of better words, "practical theology." Regrettably, many people associate this discipline with a type of crude, "hands-on" theology, or an applicational model that simply takes theories and then applies them to situations, or a realm of theology that is concerned with pastoral activities in the church. Bernard has consistently refuted these notions of practical theology and insisted that all our theologizing – whatever "brand" we prefer – must at some point be in engaged serious dialogue with the world around us. The task is "to connect the Scripture with our present experience in ways that give concrete direction to our living" (BGW, 43). Practical theology "has the same form as the structure of Christian experience: listening to God in all the ways that God speaks, listening hard to the concrete realities of our lived experience, and implementing the meanings that arise from the dialogue between them" (BGW, 10). And lest we think this task is too easily accomplished, Bernard writes: "I am convinced that Christianity is an explosion waiting to go off, a revolutionary idea still to be comprehended, a banquet in time and in history that has barely been nibbled at, and a source of social change the dimensions of which are not being dreamed of" (BGW, 58).

6. "The Roads of the Book"

Among the many thinkers Bernard has introduced to me, one especially stands out: Edmond Jabès, an unclassifiable Jewish poet-mystic-thinker. Bernard describes his first encounter with Jabès' texts in *Jesus and the Metaphors of God*: "Jabès writes about the limitations of writing, and produces non-books about the books he *would* write but, like every writer, will never write, because *that* book stays only and always in the shadows of the non-book" (JM, 6).

Bernard has authored (and co-authored) some dozen books, not to mention innumerable journal articles. He offers these works to us, his readers, as the gifts of wisdom he has gleaned from his own personal, communal and academic life. Yet he knows he will never write *that* book – and yet, it is *that* book which generates the passion and inspiration of each of Bernard's works. As a rabbinic sage notes, "You are not required to complete the task, yet neither are you free to withdraw from it" (*Pirkei Avot*, 2:21). I offer the following excerpts from Edmond Jabès because they speak to us of the labor and the gift inherent in the writings of Bernard J. Lee:

> The roads of the book are roads of instinct, listening, attention, reserve, and daring laid out by words and sustained by questions. Road toward the open.[18]

> "Writing means going on a journey, at the end of which you will not be the same," said Reb Denté.[19]

> It has the dimensions of the book and the bitter stubbornness of a wandering question.[20]

> "There is no preferential place for the book," he had written, "but there might be a non-place made up of all the thinkable places."[21]

> Between one book and the next, there is the empty space of a missing book, linked with we do not know which of the two.[22]

So ever since the book, my life has been a wake of writing in the space between limits, under the resplendent sign of the unpronounceable Name.[23]

"I have tried to be the word of the book, for the past and future of the book," Yukel said.[24]

Make allowance for fire where writing spreads . . . Ah, write, write to keep alive the fire of creation. Raise words from their peaceful night where they lay buried, words still astonished at their resurrection.[25]

You must believe in the book in order to write it. The time of writing is the time of this faith.[26]

Conclusion

In the *Preface* to *The Galilean Jewishness of Jesus,* Bernard says, "There are so many lives I might have lived besides the one I concretely live at this moment" (GJ, 1). He goes on to suggest that we should never be blithely content with the way things are, but should always be open to new possibilities and new "otherwises." And yet, each of us is also called to fulfil our particular task or vocation in the world. Just prior to his death, Rabbi Zusya said to his disciples: "In the coming world, they will not ask me: 'Why were you not Moses?' They will ask me: 'Why were you not Zusya?'"[27] Well, I think we can say that Bernard is definitely Bernard, and that in his writings and in his company, we find ourselves blessed with the wonder and astonishment of God's great love for the world – "for no good reason," other than "the goodness of God" (HJ, 98).

REFERENCES

Texts by Bernard J. Lee, S.M.

RE   *Religious Experience and Process Theology: The Pastoral Implications of a Major Modern Movement.* Co-edited with Harry James Cargas. New York: Paulist Press, 1976.

AF   *Alternative Futures for Worship: The Eucharist.* Vol. 3. Collegeville: The Liturgical Press, 1987.

GJ   *The Galilean Jewishness of Jesus: Retrieving the Jewish Origins of Christianity.* New York: Paulist Press, 1988.

JM   *Jesus and the Metaphors of God: The Christs of the New Testament.* New York: Paulist Press, 1993.

FC   *The Future Church of 140BCE: A Hidden Revolution.* New York: Crossroad, 1995.

HJ   *Habits for the Journey: A Mystical and Political Spirituality for Small Communities.* Dayton, Ohio: North American Center for Marianist Studies, 2000.

BGW   *The Beating of Great Wings: A Worldly Spirituality for Active, Apostolic Communities.* Mystic, CT: Twenty-Third Publications, 2004.

Other References

1   Malka, Salomon. 2002. *Emmanuel Levinas: His Life and Legacy.* Pittsburgh: Duquesne University Press, 124.

2   All citations in this volume are from the *New Revised Standard Version.* NY: Oxford University Press, 1991.

3   Levinas, Emmanuel. 1989. *The Levinas Reader.* Ed. Sean Hand. Oxford: Blackwell, 230.

4   Heschel, Abraham. 1965. *Who is Man?* Stanford, CA: Stanford University Press, 106.

5   Loomer, Bernard. 1976. "S-I-Z-E is the Measure," in Harry James Cargas and Bernard J. Lee, eds. *Religious Experience and Process Theology,* New York: Paulist Press, 69-76.

6   Marcel, Gabriel. 2002. *Creative Fidelity.* New York: Fordham University Press, 88.

7 Buber, Martin. 1975. *Tales of the Hasidim*. New York: Schocken Books, 89.

8 Tracy, David. 1981. *The Analogical Imagination: Christian Theology and the Plurality of Cultures*. New York: Crossroad, 382.

9 Steiner, George. 1989. *Real Presences*. Chicago: The University of Chicago Press, 143.

10 Kushner, Lawrence. 1993. *The Book of Words: Talking Spiritual Life, Living Spiritual Talk*. Woodstock, Vermont: Jewish Lights Publishing, 94.

11 Gadamer, Hans-Georg. 1989. *Truth and Method*. 2nd Rev. ed. New York: Crossroad.

12 Veling, Terry. 2005. *Practical Theology: On Earth as It Is in Heaven*. Maryknoll, NY: Orbis Books, xi.

13 Ricoeur, Paul. 1967. *The Symbolism of Evil*. Boston: Beacon Press, 348.

14 Meland, Bernard. 1953. "The Appreciative Consciousness," in *Higher Education and the Human Spirit*. Chicago: University of Chicago Press.

15 Heschel, Abraham. 1962. *The Prophets*. Vol. 2. New York: Harper Torchbooks, 263.

16 Heschel, Abraham. 2010. *Heavenly Torah: As Refracted Through the Generations*. New York: Continuum.

17 Chardin de, Teilhard. 1960. *The Divine Milieu*. New York: Harper & Row, 62.

18 Jabès, E. "There is such a thing as Jewish writing . . ." in Eric Gould, ed. *The Sin of the Book:*

Edmond Jabès. Trans. Rosmarie Waldrop. Lincoln: University of Nebraska, 1985, 29.

19 Jabès, E. *The Book of Questions*. Vol. 1. Hanover: Wesleyan University Press/ University Press of New England, 1972, 169.

20 Ibid., 26.

21 Ibid., 328.

22 Ibid., 302

23 Jabès, Edmond. 1989. *The Book of Shares*. Chicago: University of Chicago Press, 18.

24 Ibid., 3.

25 Ibid., 99

26 Jabès, Edmond. 1990. *The Book of Resemblances*. Vol.1. Hanover: Wesleyan University Press/ University Press of New England.

27 Ouaknin, M. *The Burnt Book: Reading the Talmud*. Princeton, NJ: Princeton University Press, 1995, 59

Chapter 2

Method Matters

The Role of Imagination in Theological Reflection

Evelyn and James Whitehead

Prologue: The imaginative career of Bernard Lee

T hroughout his long career Bernard Lee has attempted to enlarge our imaginations to embrace the mysterious workings of divine grace. We think immediately of three areas to which his work returned again and again. Bernard continually sought to help us imagine the enduring Hebrew influence on our Christian faith, coaxing us past two millennia of Greek – what Bernard might call logo-centric – thought. He has also repeatedly invited us to imagine a world in process. Here he was influenced by Whitehead – that would be Alfred North – in his view of an endlessly expanding world, as opposed to a static reality shaped by eternal truths. Third, through his life-long explorations of Christian communities as the holding environments of faith, Bernard has focused our imagination on the spiritual journey as a communal adventure, not simply the private pursuit of holiness.

These endeavors lead us to think more about the role of imagination in theological reflection. The importance of imagination is underscored in this season of the church's life – so in need of new ways of apprehending God's saving presence in our broken world.

We turn here to three authors, tracking their use of imagination in critical reflection. Theologian Bradford Hinze, like Bernard, locates himself at the heart of the Christian tradition. Philosopher Roberto Unger stands at the margin of our faith tradition, familiar with the language and hopes of Christian faith but directing his ideas at a larger world, a location also familiar to Bernard. Philosopher William Connelly operates well beyond the margin of Christian life but remains deeply respectful of Christian efforts to understand the present world; again, this is a position not unfamiliar to Bernard.

"Faith is a living out of the figures of hope unleashed by the imagination."

Paul Ricoeur

1972 was a very good year. Bernard Lee had just completed the programs of advanced theological study he had undertaken in two foreign countries – Fribourg, Switzerland and Berkeley, California. Influenced by the process thought of Alfred North Whitehead, he began a life-long examination of that complex and sometimes contradictory process we know as Christian tradition. Moving to the Midwest—first Missouri, then Minnesota – he began what has become his continuing exploration of the pastoral role and theological significance of small communities of faith. To all these creative efforts, Bernard brought his provocative and productive imagination. We offer this reflection on the role of imagination in theological reflection in gratitude for Bernard's creative contributions.[1]

In the 1970s, when Evelyn and I began our own exploration of the processes of theological reflection, we touched on the role of imagination only briefly. Intuitively we were aware of the significance of imagination in the life of ancient Israel: our religious ancestors were able to discern in rainbows and shifting clouds indications of God's guidance; their imaginations could envision what did not yet exist – "swords beaten into plowshares." Even then we sensed, if only partly, that the power of prophecy abides in the imagination: "Behold, I am about to do a new thing. Now it springs forth. Do you not perceive it?" (*Isaiah* 43:19) But few theologians were exploring the positive contribution of imagination to ecclesial reflection.

In the 1980s widespread interest in the imagination emerged, in both the social sciences and theology. We will trace several strands of this development. Let us begin with two questions. What does the imagination – with its capacity to generate images, symbols and metaphors – have to do with theological reflection? How does the imagination – with its ability to project unseen possibilities – contribute to the life of faith?

In 2011 Bradford Hinze published his essay "Ecclesial Impasse: What Can We Learn From Our Laments?" which brilliantly exemplifies a method of pastoral theological reflection on the contemporary life of the Church.[2] Hinze begins, as theological reflection must, by lifting up a specific area of concern – the communal experience of disappointment, dismay and disarray that pervades the Catholic Church today. This experience arises from a variety of sources: the continuing clergy sexual abuse scandal, the roll-back of Vatican II reforms in liturgy and elsewhere, the intransigent resistance of bishops to women serving in ecclesial leadership roles, and the demeaning treatment of gay and lesbian members of the church.

Impasse and lamentation

Hinze names this communal experience one of *impasse* – a concept that includes "situations of oppression, prejudice, and ecclesial struggles for reform."[3] Impasse describes the shared experience of being unable to move—whether forward or backward. People are stymied, stuck and disoriented. While this experience is filled with distress, it also offers an opportunity: impasse can serve as "a crucible for desire, reason, memory and imagination."[4] Here Hinze offers his first hint concerning the role of imagination in theological reflection.

He then identifies this group experience at a deeper level: the current impasse can be seen through the biblical lens of lamentation. Here Hinze rescues the contemporary experience from its historical isolation, linking present distress with the profound tradition of lament: our religious ancestors lifting up their grief-stricken hearts to God, protesting in loud complaint.

"At its core, lament expresses the pain of unfulfilled aspirations or intentions. The reasons for pain may be limitations or failings, personal or collective, singular or compound, episodic or chronic; but whatever the cause (named or nameless, known or hidden from consciousness), the result is an ache, tension, rage, dissipation of energy, a numbness, all of which contribute to the state that Walter Brueggemann has aptly described as disorientation."[5]

Hinze acknowledges that the mood of desolation and lament threatens to disrupt the community's life. "Laments can signal disorder and destructive dynamics at work in the Church." (494) Yet he argues that grieving may be the work of the Spirit, compelling us to examine and release aspects of our life of faith that no longer serve, that have hardened into rigid understandings and dysfunctional structures. A time of impasse may then serve as "a crucible of the imagination," when "the social imaginary provided by ecclesial memory can be insufficient to address ...the signs of the times." (488)

The social imaginary and the sense of the faithful

Bradford Hinze suggests that "testimonies of lament [may be] disclosing new aspirations of the *sensus fidelium* of the Church that build on what had previously been taught and practiced and bring into view a challenging new perception of the truth of the gospel." (494)

Hinze then places this traditional *sensus fidelium*, an image resurrected in the Vatican II document on the Church, in touch with Charles Taylor's understanding of a social imaginary. A time of impasse in the church today may register an evolving sense of the faithful that challenges a "social imaginary provided by ecclesial memory (which) can be insufficient to address impasse and the signs of the times." (488) Here Hinze raises several challenges: first, he suggests that the sense of the faith may be more than a rhetorical consensus concerning Christian belief; it may function as a more dynamic and evolving intuition that is "disclosing new aspirations." Second, the established "ecclesial memory" of how the life of faith is to proceed may be found to be "insufficient" to address current challenges. A traditional social imaginary, shaped by earlier concerns, may be unable to read "the signs of the times."

Charles Taylor defines the social imaginary as the way in which a particular group of people "imagine their social existence, how they fit together with others, how things go on between them and their fellows, the expectations that are normally met..."[6] A social imaginary is the self-awareness of a particular culture, enshrined in specific images of social life, moral obligation, individuality, religion. This constellation of *orientations* – of beliefs and biases, of convictions and concerns – serves

20

as "an implicit map of social space" and forms the collective identity of that group. This shared view of communal life is more than a theory or abstract worldview. The social imaginary is "carried in images, stories, and legends,"[7] and "makes possible common practices, and a widely shared sense of legitimacy."[8]

The implicit structure of a social imaginary become more obvious when its *taken for granted* character begins to be questioned. A long-honored, widely shared sense of legitimacy begins to give way; a traditional way of organizing social life is no longer persuasive. Common practices – of loyalty to traditional leaders or of adherence to religious faith – are no longer compelling.

In the Vatican II document on the Church (*Lumen Gentium*; "Light of the World," paragraph twelve) the bishops recalled this ancient conviction that the faith community as a whole actively possesses a vibrant and reliable appreciation of core religious belief and practice.

> Thanks to a supernatural sense of faith which characterizes the People as a whole, it manifests this unerring quality when 'from the bishops down to the last member of the laity,' it shows universal agreement in matters of faith and morals.

This sense of faith, couched here in a hierarchical setting ("from the bishops down..."), and assumed to reach an idealistic "universal agreement," is subsequently described as a more dynamic reality. It is a sense of faith that "clings without fail to a faith once delivered by the Saints, penetrates it more deeply by accurate insights, and applies it more thoroughly to life." The progression in the verbs – *clings* [a conservative embrace], *penetrates* [a more active analysis], *applies* [a contemporary, practical expression] – suggests development and even transformation at play in a faith community's deepening sense of faith.[9]

Imagination and method

Impasse brings us to a halt and defeats our current mode of operation: rational analysis bogs down; planning techniques and corporate strategizing stall. The mind and heart are forced to turn to the imagination, to the domain of intuition and symbols. Hinze suggests that imagination may provide the ordinary path to find our way through an impasse. God works this transformation in our souls; from self-composure and control, through the disorientations that accompany the sense of losing our way, and then to new hopes arising in the imagination.

Hinze recognizes imagination as a human capacity manifest throughout the Scriptures but with little legitimacy in contemporary ecclesial life. But its power can be reclaimed; the community of faith has been here before. As we view our contemporary distress through the lens of biblical imagery, we may be able to see "situations of lamentation as experiences of impasse (that) provide the fertile soil for the power of God to work in the imagination." (489) Grieving understandings of faith and of structures of church life that no longer serve, a people may "find passage through the intense furnace of laments that will destroy idols and distorted views of the self and community as it transforms our memories and imagination in the work of God." (489) And, the "intense furnace of laments" unleashed in this impasse compels a transformation of "our memories and imagination."

Having focused attention on the imagination, Hinze turns to questions of method. He points to the need for "a theology and hermeneutic of lamentation as an indispensable facet in ecclesiological method and in our pastoral practices by means of synodal processes of discernment." (491) But he wonders: how are we "to make room …for individuals and communities to express their own laments about everyday ecclesial and social life?" (485) Expressed another way, "is there *a pastoral communal process* for personal and communal laments to be articulated and heard in synods, dioceses, and parishes?" (486)

In this call for a contemporary method of theological reflection, Hinze emphasizes the importance of the "public sphere." He stresses the need to "create a public space for the people of God—not just the descendants of the apostles, martyrs, and ascetics, but all the faithful – to speak up for themselves and voice their own laments." Charles Taylor has discussed the contemporary importance of such a public sphere or civic space: "It is a space of discussion which is self-consciously seen as being outside power. It is supposed to be listened to by power, but it is not itself an exercise of power." In other words, "with the modern public sphere comes the idea that political power must be supervised and checked by something outside. What was new, of course, was not that there was an outside check, but rather the nature of this instance. It is not defined as the will of God, or the Law of Nature (although it could be thought to articulate these), but as a kind of discourse, emanating from reason and not from power or traditional authority."[10] How such a public sphere might be carved out within the church, but distinct from its designated authority structure, remains to be seen.

More time and talent than is available here is required to play out the inevitable tension between an evolving sense of the faithful (beset with laments) and an entrenched social structure representative of an earlier era and with little trust in "a (democratic) public sphere."[11] Tragedy ensues when church leaders cling to a social mindset anchored in a lost world.

Hinze concludes his essay on a more hopeful note: "But we need to be mindful that when cries are too deep for words, there the agitating agency of the Spirit can also be at work. The lodestars in the process of discernment may be peace, joy, and compassion, but the energy fields that give birth to new galaxies and supernovas, new constellations in the Church and in the world are laments." (495)

For Hinze the imagination plays a crucial role in theological reflection. Yet the question remains: what is this interior resource and how does it function in a life of faith?

****

Interlude # 1: What is the imagination?

We find ourselves with the peculiar capacity to reflect on times and places that do not exist. We can envision a future that is not yet; we are able to forgive the past – a considerable feat of the imagination. We can even picture the unlikely possibility of weapons being reshaped into plows. (Isaiah 2:4) The imagination is a curious capability that anchors our moral and religious lives, and plays a key role in theological reflection.

Psychologists are researching the emergence of this evolved capacity in the physiology of the brain. Evolutionary psychologist Daniel Gilbert writes: "The greatest achievement of the human brain is its ability to imagine

23

objects and episodes that do not exist in the realm of the real, and it is this ability that allows us to think about the future. If nature has given us a greater gift, no one has named it."[12]

Theologian Craig Dykstra writes, "The human imagination is the integrating process that provides linkages between ourselves and the world – and, within ourselves, between our bodies, minds and emotions, our very souls and spirits. It is by means of the imagination that we are able to come really to see and understand anything at all – even, in a sense, to see God."[13]

Centuries before psychology appeared as an academic discipline, Thomas Aquinas offered his estimation of the importance of imagination: "The image is the principle of our knowledge. It is that from which the intellectual activity begins, not as a passing stimulus, but as an enduring foundation. When the imagination is choked, so also is our theological knowledge."[14]

We leave the last word here to Paul Ricoeur. "Imagination can be described as a rule-governed form of invention" and "the power of re-describing reality." And, perhaps of greatest importance, "The discipline of reality is nothing without the grace of imagination."[15]

****

A view from the margin: Method and imagination

Brazilian-born philosopher Roberto Unger, a longtime member of the faculty of the Harvard University Law School, has for decades explored the enduring tensions of the human experience. In his earlier work, *Passion: An Essay on Personality* (1984), he examined an essential paradox: "we present to one another both an unlimited need and unlimited danger" (20). He identifies this tension as the drama of longing and jeopardy. Our endless desire and need for one another is matched by the unending fear of being injured or manipulated or overwhelmed by the other. As guides through this impasse, Unger offers the "ennobling passions" of faith, hope and love.[16]

In a more recent work, *The Self Awakened* (2007), Unger broadens the lens of his analysis to examine the social tension of our lives. He understands personal experience as necessarily contextualized by institutions and their methods, yet able to – and often eager to – transcend these limiting frameworks. Our identity as embodied spirits is essentially shaped by this enduring tension between structures that provide continuity and safety to our fragile lives and the constant need to escape and/or transcend these boundaries.[17]

"The single idea that resounds on every page of this book is the idea of the infinity of the human spirit, in the individual as well as humanity. It is a view of the wonderful and terrible disproportion of that spirit to everything that would contain and diminish it..." (26-27)

Unger repeatedly recognizes "the wonderful and terrible disproportion of that spirit to everything that would contain and diminish it." And, "Our powers of insight outreach our capacities for proof." (p.8) And again, "in the life of desire, we find at every turn that our most intense longings, attachments, and addictions constantly transcend their immediate objects."

Questions of method

Caught in this everlasting tension, how shall we proceed? What method of reflection will best support such embodied spirits? Unger offers this guidance: "Our activities fall into two classes. Some activities are moves *within a framework* of organization and belief that we take for granted. At the limit, the framework remains unchallenged and even invisible. We naturalize or sanctify it, treating as natural fact or sacred imperative the collective product of our own hands." (56)

Unger then points to an alternate method of reflection, one with more revolutionary potential. "Other activities are moves *about the framework*. Such activities change the framework the only way it ordinarily can be changed: piece by piece and step by step." (56) He then compares "context-preserving activities" with "context-transforming activities." These parallel the alternation of routine and repetition (essential to every life) versus the novel. "Repetition frees energy and time for what we do not yet know how to repeat." (56) Repetition serves the routinized parts of our lives, but predictably serves more as barrier when we are confronted with the novel, the unexpected, or "what we do not yet know how to repeat." Here vision and imagination are essential tools to free us from repetition and open us to the new.

In *Passion*, his earlier work, Unger mused on the ways that habits and routine often encase a person in unimaginative repetition. This often leads to our experiences of becoming "enslaved to an imagination spellbound by a narrow conception of possible states of existence." (163)

And while some pattern of systematic reflection is essential to any communal life, we must be able at times to access new insights that may call into question our customary ways of proceeding. "Only by the painful triumph of vision over method, the periodic subversion of method for the sake of deepening vision, can we hope to advance insight." (232) When we fail at this, our encasement in prescribed ways of behaving ends as "a species of the surrender of spirit to structure, the slow and repeated dying to which we are all subject." (233)

"The imagination is the scout of the will."

Methods of reflection that rely on repetition – re-doing what we have found previously to serve us well – are essential in life. Unger agrees that we "must use repetition, embodied in standardized practice and in machines, to save time for what is not yet repeatable." (227) But he insists that a viable method of communal reflection must remain open to the imagination – that "scout of the will" which serves us best by "anticipating how we might get to the *there*—or to different *theres*—from here. "(125)

When methodical repetition is the only mode of reflection available to us, we are likely to face necessary changes only when driven by crises. "Only when there is a crisis – that is to say, a problem for which the established structure offers no ready-made solution – do we hit against the limits of our present ideas and methods. Only then does the search for alternate ways of thinking begin. However, in thought as in social life, a mark of experimentalism is that we do not need to wait for crisis. The imagination does the work of crisis without crisis, making it possible for us to experience change without undergoing ruin." (112) Earlier in this volume Unger recorded this conviction in another of his typical formulations: when imagination is an active resource, "transformation will become less dependent on calamity." (57)

Unger then makes his strongest claim for imagination's service in a season of change: "to solve problems in the way it does, *the mind must also be able to make moves it never made before,* according to rules it can formulate, if at all, only after making them. It must, in other words, be capable of not repeating itself." What would this jarring statement mean in the context of Christian faith? To be sure, the first followers of Jesus were confronted with the demand to make decisions that set them on paths never before taken. Were these new Christians to understand their prayerful table gatherings as complementary to attendance at the synagogue or as replacing it? And more recently, in the opening sessions of the Second Vatican Council Pope John XXIII urged the attending prelates to consider decisions that would move the church in directions never before considered. And, as might have been anticipated, several of his strong recommendations —for instance, his invitation to see our Jewish ancestors in a more benevolent light – met with considerable opposition.[18]

Traditional methods of reflection, employed repetitively, gain a familiarity and authority that can easily harden into a style that outlaws novelty and risk. Institutions by their very nature enshrine beliefs in routinized rituals and authoritative dogma. These may so become embalmed in tradition that little vitality or mystery survives. How then does a religious institution, deeply committed to the survival of its well-honed structures, become "capable of not repeating itself"?

It is here that Unger offers his definition of imagination. "This impulse of surprise, invention and transcendence…turns consciousness into what we call imagination. It counts for much in the power of the mind to address the problems of action-oriented experience." (68) Later, he describes the role of the imagination as "exploring what the established methods and discourses do not allow to be thought and said." (233) Imagination invites us, in the midst of highly routinized and repetitive patterns, to take steps in directions we have never before explored. Yet for us the question remains: how will religious faith and imagination build this partnership?

****

Interlude # 2: Faith as a Way of Imagining the World

Religious faith is a way of imagining the world. Believing that our world was created and is now sustained by a loving Creator – who is present yet invisible – takes a strong imagination. This is not to suggest that faith is a fantasy or a mere figment of our mind. It is to recognize that religious faith is a God-given ability to envision the world in a particular and powerful fashion.

From the beginning this has been the case. When our religious ancestors, having escaped slavery in Egypt, found themselves lost in the desert some began to dream of "a land flowing with milk and honey." This ideal existed first only in their imaginations, fevered perhaps by the heat of the desert, but it was a hope that became a reality.

As our ancestors settled into their new land, they were reminded that their faith demanded an extraordinary feat of the imagination. "You shall not oppress a resident alien; you know the heart of an alien, for you were aliens in the land of Egypt." (Exodus 23:9) The bible turns repeatedly to the themes of the other, the alien and the stranger. The scriptural invitation to imagine the world in a more generous fashion reaches a highpoint in the story of the disciples returning home to Emmaus. The stranger they meet on the road and welcome to their table suddenly radiated the face of the risen Christ. The recognition has been like a flash – a sudden epiphany. The story of Emmaus moves us today because we too have recognized in blessed moments – our imaginations having been tutored by this story – that the stranger, the resident alien, the vulnerable outsider bears the face of Christ.

Walter Brueggemann connects faith and imagination this way: the biblical revelation is "an act of faithful imagination that buoyantly and defiantly mediates a counter-world that is a wondrous demanding alternative to the world immediately and visibly at hand."[19]

✳✳

A view from beyond the margin: Method and imagination

Philosopher William Connolly, faculty member of Johns Hopkins University, has long been involved in questions of modernity and secularity. Connelly is convinced that theories of universal or "natural" moral law, derived from Augustinian and Kantian roots, are no longer applicable. In a recent work,[20] he describes a secular approach to morality, an ethic of cultivation to replace the traditional morality of a (supposed) universal law. His intent is to provide a way of proceeding that does not depend of the explicit influence of transcendent sources. Yet at the same time he acknowledges the importance of efforts to "restore belief in the world" and advocates an "existential gratitude" for the universe we are given.[21]

Connelly's essay begins with a description of the intellectual perspective that dominates contemporary consciousness. This is a vision of "a world not intrinsically designed for either human benefit or human mastery." (98) Such a world is "neither deeply providential nor receptive to consummate human mastery." (97) These are the defining characteristics of a secular world-view: "An enlarged minority of people must embrace a vision of the world that is neither providentially ordered, teeming with gods, governed by universal moral laws, susceptible to consummate mastery, nor lodged on a secure trajectory of linear progress." (108)

A Method of moral reflection: Discern, dramatize, join forces

For Connelly a method of reflection begins in practical wisdom and requires a fresh understanding of the will. In his usage, *will* is not the traditional human faculty marked by the stain of original sin. He suggests that *will*, once "decriminalized" (that is, removed from this theological interpretation of its inherent wound) can be embraced as a vibrant inner resource – "as an emergent, bio-cultural formation, which bears traces and marks of that from which it emerged but is not reducible to them." (109)

Many of the will's tendencies to action (inclinations discussed by other authors as "moral intuitions," such as fairness, compassion, gratitude) exist below the threshold of full conscious control. This insight suggests the basic orientation required for effective moral reflection. "The initial drive is to amplify, by whatever modes of cultivation available, preliminary strains of care for the earth and the vitality of life already circulating to some degree in and between most people much of the time. The idea is to fold those predispositions more actively into established patterns of desire, faith, identity, and self-interest rather than to rise to a disinterested level above the mundane worlds of desire, instrumentality, and politics." (110)

Turning then to the method of reflection, Connelly outlines three movements. The first requirement is "to listen more closely than you have heretofore for aspirations and understandings by others that have escaped you and to chords of attachment you may have missed." In an earlier essay he described this initial stance as the "agonistic respect" to be accorded one's intellectual adversaries: "a relation of respectful connection across difference and competition...reciprocal appreciation of the deep contestability" of many questions.[22]

Having listened respectfully to others, one must then "dramatize this seed of existential attachment so that it might grow further." (This movement is similar to the stage of assertion in the tri-polar method of pastoral reflection we have developed: the effort required to express or witness to one's own beliefs and convictions). The third challenge is "to join forces with others to resist the most ruthless attempts to foreclose diversity or to sacrifice the future of the earth to the demands of the present." (111)

Dramatization is key in Connelly's method. He is convinced that the age of confident rational demonstrations of universal laws is long past. Our task instead is more humble: the effort to discern the moral intuitions that might protect and advance the life we share with other living things on this small planet. Then the challenge to *dramatize* – as we try to show convincingly why such a vision is compelling. In such an effort, "persuasion...attraction and inspiration" will be part of this effort. Moral discourse, long assumed to be driven by rational insight, is acknowledged now as more an aesthetic adventure – the dramatic and imaginative portrayal of the good life as we see it. [23]

Critical reflection: A new demand

The cultivation of such a moral stance is not enough. In a world undergoing enormous changes, our method must embrace yet another discipline, one that Connelly names "periodic hesitation." This is a disciplined pause that allows us to exist in "the gap between a new disturbance and prior investment of habit, passion, faith, identity, progress, and political priority." (111) In the ancient Greek world, those proficient in this discipline were called seers; in ancient Israel they were named prophets. Such a discipline allows us to be attentive to "untimely ideas" which emerge—often half hidden—among us. In what Connelly calls "exercises in dwelling" a reflective method should allow "latent memories, established codes, care for being, existential worries, and emerging pressures to resonate back and forth, almost mindlessly." (112) Although Connelly does not explicitly employ the term *imagination* in his discussion, we can recognize this resource at play. It is imagination that mutes the default movements of rational scrutiny and critical judgment.

In *A World Becoming*, Connolly expands on this heuristic movement he identifies as the "fecundity of hesitation." He describes a "fecund moment of dwelling in duration that punctuates the secular time of everyday perception, judgment and action." During such a moment," he continues, "multiple layers of the past resonate with things unfolding in the current situation, sometimes issuing in something new – as if from nowhere. The *new* is ushered into being through a process that exceeds rational calculation or the derivation of practical implications from universal principles." (69)

Connelly offers a striking example of such fruitful hesitation: he recalls the gospel scene in which Jesus confronts a mob preparing to stone a woman caught in adultery. Jesus' first response is one of silence; he stoops down and begins to write on the ground. But the bystanders insist that the Mosaic Law calls for stoning in this instance. Jesus responds, "Let the person who is without sin cast the first stone." And then he again bends down and continues his writing.

Connelly imaginatively expands the scenario of Jesus' silent response. "As Jesus stoops and draws dreamily on the ground with his finger, he may allow the indignity of his earthly conception, the same born by an unwed mother, the plight of his people under the yoke of empire, the danger of the vengeful crowd, the Mosaic code he and they have absorbed, the acute danger facing the accused woman before him, and his own unconventional relation to Mary Magdalene to mingle in a crystal of time. A new maxim crystallizes, as these layers of memory, pressure, and concern reverberate in a distinctive situation. Care for the world, informed by exquisite sensitivity to an unpredictable moment, merely set conditions of possibility for it." (69)

What Jesus had done in this instance was to "stop the clock" that was measuring the rush to righteous judgment. In this interval – as customary conviction is held in check – the imagination opens space for other thoughts, other conclusions.

For Connelly the special challenge is to devise strategies to include this moment of pause into any method of critical reflection – "how to enter into moments of suspension to allow creative thoughts to gestate when a new fork in time emerges" and how to "dwell in fecund periods of withdrawal from action at some times and to intervene in ongoing practices at others."[24] Here we find affinity with Hinze's call for attentiveness to "signs of the times." In his essay, Hinze urged the community of faith to "create a public space for the people of God" to confront their grief, as well as "a pastoral communal process" that allows room for the public expression of lamentation.

✳✳✳

Interlude # 3: Prophecy and imagination

"Behold, I am about to do a new thing. Now it springs forth. Do you not perceive it?" (Isaiah 43:19)

The vocation of the prophet depends on the gift of imagination. Throughout the Hebrew Scriptures, prophets resorted to this dramatic resource to awaken their people to renewal. Jeremiah trudged through Jerusalem carrying a yoke to demonstrate the future bondage into which the Jewish people would fall. Isaiah, fatigued by war, pictured swords being beaten into plows. This transformation, so unlikely then and now, appeared first in his imagination; it still fires hearts of peacemakers today. Walter Brueggemann: "The vocation of the prophet was to keep alive the ministry of the imagination, to keep on conjuring and proposing alternative futures to the single one the king wants to urge as the only thinkable one."[25]

The role of the prophet is to show a believing community God's future. Jesus was in this line of prophets, speaking repeatedly of the reign of God about to break into reality. He told his followers of its signs: the blind see and the lame walk upright. He insisted that this hopeful reality was already "among them." But where, we might ask? In their imaginations, as promise of a world of justice and peace that could become real.

In the course of the Third Century the ministry of prophets gradually disappeared from the life of the church. With it went a confidence in the imagination. Henceforth, church leaders, convinced that revelation was

32

now complete, argued that obedience would assume pride of place. The religious imagination survived of course, both within the church (in the mystics, such as Theresa of Avila and John of the Cross) and outside its defined orthodoxy (in dissidents and reformers, such as Luther and Calvin). In the face of the challenges of secularism in a late-modern world, Hinze, Unger and Connelly speak of the imagination as an essential resource for the future.

✳✳✳

Re-imagining our grief: Lamentation and resentment

"It is my grief – that the right hand of the Most High has changed." (Psalms 77: 10)

In his method of theological reflection Bradford Hinze seeks to bring the painful impasse experienced in the Catholic Church these days into explicit focus. By naming this experience as lament, he links present distress with Scriptural memories of Israel's grief and lamentation. This connection awakens the religious imagination to ancient strategies of lament. In the midst of their suffering, our religious ancestors turned private pain into public expression; they transformed pain into prayer. With this tactic they avoided the temptations of any social crisis—compelling pain to remain hidden as private distress or to let it explode vindictively in blame of other people. At lamentation's core is the confident belief that God knows our plight, hears our prayers, will bring us through to a better life—scalded perhaps but cleansed.

In her study of the biblical text of *The Book of Lamentation*, Kathleen O'Connor describes the mysterious dynamic of grief in Scripture and in our lives. "Lamentation can shred the heart and spawn despair, but, paradoxically, by mirroring pain it can also comfort the afflicted and open the way toward healing. It can affirm the dignity of those who suffer, release their tears, and overcome their experience of abandonment."[26]

Institutional leaders may prefer to foreclose on communal lament by keeping pain private. A faithful woman's desire to serve the community as an ordained priest is simply dismissed as the (misguided) experience of an individual. The scandal of clerical sexual abuse is explained as a matter of individual guilt, leaving unexamined the contribution of traditional structures of ecclesiastical leadership. The gay couple's request for a public ceremony to celebrate their commitment is likewise seen as an inappropriate individual demand. Privatizing these movements of desire and regret as simply expressions of individual concern keeps a community from recognizing how widespread are such laments.

William Connelly examines a quite different response to collective grief – what he names "existential resentment."[27] Connelly identifies this distress as a destructive force in US society today. This toxic reaction emerges as more than temporary personal pain. Connelly refers to this disturbance as "a dangerous temptation built into the human condition itself," (113) a toxic mood that is "always simmering as a possibility in mortals who must come to terms with the issues of mortality, economic inequality, suffering, sickness, exploitation, and fundamental misfortune." (61)

Connelly acknowledges that resentment often begins in a focused distress: the loss of a job or mortgage foreclosure or both. Grief then escalates into a wider disappointment, reflected in the polls that show a growing number of citizens unhappy with the direction of the country. An expanding agitation, encouraged by talk show hosts and fundamentalist preachers, mushrooms into a pervasive anger (Connelly sees this as the emotion's "existential" quality) that looks for someone to blame.

Connelly cautions that this developing "spirituality of resentment" often motivates "tactics of revenge against vulnerable constituencies whose very existence poses a threat to your self-confidence and self-assurance." (61) Unlike the lamentation that our biblical ancestors learned to turn into prayer, this contemporary unrest is "infused with existential resentment…(that) fosters a spirit of punitiveness toward diversity and a refusal to give a degree of priority to the future over the present." (108) As antidote, Connelly urges cultivating an abiding gratitude for the extravagant generosity of the world "so that the insidious spirit of *ressentiment* does not seep into the inner core of our being, dividing us too profoundly against ourselves, and encouraging us to search too actively for collective enemies." (81)

In *A Secular Age* Charles Taylor refers to this destructive social mood as "a bellicose spirituality" that fuels "the evangelical-capitalist resonance machine" in the United States these days. He sees evangelicals and free marketers joining forces in their focused efforts to amplify social resentment. (143) Taylor argues that this is a "resentment of the world for not possessing either providence or ready susceptibility to human mastery." (135) Such a toxic emotion, spreading contagiously through a culture, displaces both gratitude and genuine lamentation.

Conclusion

Over his scholarly career Bernard Lee has championed the role of imagination in enlivening efforts to fathom our life with God. In our imaginations we gather together the disparate events of our past into a plot with direction and purpose. Through the prism of inspired imagination deserts and exiles are reconfigured as way stations on a miraculous journey.

With imagination we also make sense of present distress – the impasses that mark the journey today. Through imagination our sorrow is transformed into graceful grieving rather than toxic resentment.

With imagination we envision an extraordinary future, in which we – and the community of faith – may "make moves we have never made before." Through the prism of imagination we dare to "dwell in fecund withdrawal," attentive to God's future and the flickering intimations of the coming reign of God.

Endnotes

1   Theologian Elizabeth Johnson's work on theological reflection is an excellent example of the advances made in this area. Her working definition of theological reflection: "the process unfolds from religious experience among an active community in a particular context, to popular and critically trained theological reflection, to continuing practical action arising from spiritual and moral commitment. Insight develops, in a word, from heart to head to hand." See p. 2 of her 2007 book, *Quest for the Living God*. A new interest in theological reflection arose in the 1970s as a result of the reforms of Vatican II. See, for instance, Bernard Lonergan's *Method in Theology* (Herder and Herder, 1972), David Tracy, *Blessed Rage for Order* (Seabury, 1975) and Ann Carr, "Theology and Experience in the Thought of Karl Rahner," in *Journal of Religion* 53 (July, 1973).

2   Bradford Hinze, "Ecclesial Impasse: What Can We Learn From Our Laments?" in *Theological Studies*, 72 (2011), 470-95.

3   Hinze, 2011, 486.

4   Hinze, 2011, 487.

5   Hinze, 2011, 487.

6   Charles Taylor, *A Secular Age*, p. 171.

7   Charles Taylor, *Modern Social Imaginaries*, p. 23.

8   P. 172 of *A Secular Age*.

9   This notion of a *sensus fidelium* joined other ideals released at this council. The council embraced a new and broader sense of participation: the collegiality of bishops working actively together with the bishop of Rome instead of merely applying his dictates; the ministerial collaboration among clergy and laity in parishes and other communities of faith. These new ideals, in fact, describe the emergence of a new social imaginary – or an ancient one that was rooted in the dramatic biblical passage describing a community of faith where "there is no longer Jew or Greek, there is no longer slave or free; there is no longer male or female;; for all of you are one in Christ." (Galatians 3:28) But this was a fragile imaginary of a community of equals where privilege and status had been erased; initially there were no significant social structures to ensure its survival. It existed in this first iteration at the Council as just rhetoric. And – this is the point of Hinze's essay and its emphasis on lament – since then it has failed to find expression beyond rhetoric.

10   Taylor, *Modern Social Imaginaries*, p. 25

11   After the Council, the church experimented briefly with a "public space" where married couples were invited to share with the hierarchy their seasoned convictions about various methods of birth control. Their suggestions were turned down and the space vanished with the publication of *Humanae Vitae* in 1968.

12   Daniel Gilbert's observation is quoted in Susan Neiman's *Moral Clarity*, p. 202.

13   See p. 49 of Craig Dykstra's essay, "Pastoral and Ecclesial Imagination," in *For Life Abundant*, (eds) Dorothy Bass and Craig Dykstra, Grand Rapids, Michigan, Eerdsmans, 2008.

14   See Thomas Aquinas, *Opusculum,* 16 De Trinitate. 6.2 ad 5, quoted in Margaret Miles' *Image as Insight*, p. 142.

15   See Paul Ricoeur, *Freud and Philosophy*, p. 551.

16   Roberto Unger, *Passion: An Essay in Personality.* Unger describes "the boundlessness of our need" for one another," and the paradox that whatever we receive and give to one another "seems like an advance on a spiritual transaction that we are unable to complete." (p. 96). And he writes of "our inability to find satisfaction anywhere except in the presence of other context-transcending and insatiable beings like ourselves." (p.25)

Unger's newer book is *The Self Awakened*, (Harvard University Press, 2000). We have developed his discussion of the ennobling passions of faith, hope and charity in our book, *Nourishing the Spirit: The Healing Emotions of Joy, Wonder, Compassion and Hope*, (Orbis, 2012).

17 In this new volume, Unger returns, again and again, to two opposing orientations to the question "what should I do with my life?" One answer counsels: stay out of trouble and seek serenity; the other favors getting into trouble and honoring vulnerability. An ethic driven by the goal of serenity will encourage composure and detachment "from vain striving in a world of shadowy appearances." (252) This will, in turn, lead to "a posture of detached and distance benevolence...love as kindness, whenever possible from afar and from above." (253)

With the other option – favoring getting into trouble and recognizing vulnerability – "the goal is no longer composure. It is to live a larger life, for ourselves and others" in which "we must look for trouble" in order to change the world. Serenity – the ideal of the Stoics that has found its way into much Christian piety – counsels caution and detachment. The ideal of honoring our vulnerability invites risk – a willingness to lose our composure – and attachment to other vulnerable companions.

18 Elizabeth Groppe examines the changing theology of the Jewish people in Vatican II and the resistance to this new understanding, in her essay, "Revisiting Vatican II's Theology of The People of God after Forty-five Years of Catholic –Jewish Dialogue," in *Theological Studies*, 72 (2011), 586-619.

19 Walter Brueggemann defines biblical faith in See Walter Brueggemann, *The Prophetic Imagination*, p. 45, and his "Imaginative remembering" in his *An Introduction to the Old Testament* (Louisville, KT: Westminster John Knox, 2003), p. 21.

20 See his essay, "Shock Therapy, Dramatization, and Practical Wisdom," in *The Joy of Secularism*, (ed) George Levine, Princeton University Press, 2011. 95-114). Also see his *A World of Becoming*, (Durham, NC: Duke University Press, 2011).

21 In his most recent book, *A World of Becoming*, Connelly describes the peculiar secularity to which he subscribes: "A world of becoming can be enchanted in some ways, even if it does not express divine meanings that are partly revealed and partly hidden, and even if it is not a providential world. For a world of becoming is marked by surprising turns in time, uncanny experiences, and the possibility of human participation to some degree in larger processes of creativity that both include and surpass the human estate." (70)

22 Connolly, in an essay on "Catholicism and Philosophy, A Nontheistic Appreciation," in *Charles Taylor*, develops his notion of respect for those we do not agree with. He writes: "Agonistic respect means a relation of respectful connection across difference and competition…reciprocal appreciation of the deep contestability" of many questions. (167)

"Agonistic respect is expressed in the way you engage faiths that bypass the source you honor most fervently; it thereby finds expression in the way you represent the beliefs, practices, and ideals of your adversaries." (180)

23 In *A world of Becoming*, Connelly summarizes his method of critical reflection: "Experience, experiment, reflection, cultivation of spiritual sensibility, and resolute action are five dimensions that cannot stray far from each other." (p. 10)

24 *Ibid.*, p. 15. Author Hanif Kureishi provides a gloss on this discipline and its relation to a method with his remarks on "The Art of Distraction," *The New York Times*, Sunday, Feb. 19, 2012. He observes that "some interruptions are worth having if they create a space for something to work in the fertile unconscious." He adds, "you could say that attention needs to be paid to intuition: one can learn to attend to the hidden self, and there might be something there worthy listening to…a flighty mind might be going somewhere." He ends by linking such disciplined "distractions" with method: "In the end, a person requires a method. He must be able to distinguish between creative and destructive distractions by the sort of taste they leave, whether they feel depleting or fulfilling. And this can work only if he is, as much as possible, in good communication with himself – if he is, as it were, on his own side, caring for himself imaginatively, an artist of his own life."

25 Brueggemann, p. 45 of *The Prophetic Imagination*.

26 Kathleen O'Connor's *Lamentation and the Tears of the World*, p. 96.

27 Connolly links his discussion of resentment with Nietzsche's famous accusation of Christianity as rooted in this toxic mood, and with sociologist Max Scheler's exploration of this emotion. Scheler suggested that resentment arises when a person is angered at an authority that he cannot confront. This distress is swallowed and turns to thoughts of revenge. For Scheler, "*ressentiment* is a self-poisoning of the mind…a lasting mental attitude, caused by the systematic repression of certain emotions." He adds, "Revenge tends to be transformed into *ressentiment* the more it is directed against lasting situations, which are felt to be injurious but beyond one's control – in other words, the more the injury is experienced as destiny." (p. 121 of Max Scheler, *On Feeling, Knowing, and Valuing*, (Chicago: University of Chicago Press, 1992). The writer Malachi McCourt has given perhaps the most succinct definition of resentment: "taking poison and waiting for the other person to die."

Chapter 3

"And your bones will flourish like the new grass"[1]

Process Thought and Social Commitment

Nancy Dallavalle

Introduction

Whitehead's wide-ranging contributions left an important mark on the adventurous ideas he so happily engaged over six decades as a mathematician and philosopher, making notable contributions to metaphysics and the philosophy of science (although the researcher seeking a comprehensive overview of his work will soon find that she's off on a scavenger hunt of the entire library). While there continues to be a "Whiteheadian school" within Christian theology, energized by Claremont School of Theology's Center for Process Studies, it is a tribute to the plasticity and usefulness of the insights he developed that they turn up, unannounced, with far greater regularity than a citation count would reveal. Bernard Lee's theological work, which includes substantial contributions to the field of practical and pastoral theology, has furthered this trajectory in both its explicit and implicit forms.

In appreciation for the numerous contributions of Bernard Lee, this essay will (I.) highlight two aspects of that approach: its commitment to concrete fact and its willingness to take flight from that fact in favor of a vision of human community that is both radically inclusive and composed of real people, and then consider the appearance of novelty as a necessary element for this vision. This essay's constructive contribution (II.) will then explore some recent theological uses of Whitehead's thought as these bear upon our notions of God and community, with a special eye for how descriptions of these come to bear on the development of intermediary structures characterized by resilience and change and novelty, as the current moment calls us to new and flexible forms that will sustain life-giving communities.

I. Intellectual commitments

Whitehead's metaphysics has proven to be a fertile cosmology for both philosophers and theologians. While several theologians are still directly engaged with his sense of reality as a series of events, and continue to think through traditional religious claims, East and West, with the technical vocabulary of *Process and Reality*, Whitehead's stronger impact on theology has been in the broader dissemination of his sensibility. This sensibility critiques the fundamental claim of classical theology, and has led most fruitfully to empirical and pragmatic schools of liberal theology.

Lee finds these two to be useful guides for good theological work. The empirical strand is based on the work of Dewey and Pierce, and argues for a radical empiricism as a strong counter for what seems to be a disembodied sense of the rational in Greek thought. This radical empiricism, Lee argues, more adequately serves the retrieval of the Hebrew character of the community gathered around Jesus – and, indeed, this community is the focus of his book on the Jewishness of Jesus.[2] Such an empiricism includes an emphasis on an historically accurate account of Jesus and Nazareth and Christian origins, one that will insist that this account shake loose the accretions of Christian claims as these have shaped the narrative about Jesus – to the point of obscuring, in the end, his own religious faith. This approach focuses on what can be found to be the "facts of the matter," theologically claiming that revelation must begin with what actually happened.

Moreover, this historical and empirical approach will assume that the product of this reflection will be a "natural theology," one that will think through the categories of Jesus and the church in a way that does not depend on a fideistic sense of revelation. In Bernard Lee's hands, however, this approach is not confined, but robust. With process thought, he will judge "classical theism" to be not necessarily incorrect, but rather deficient, in its metaphysical claim that there is a non-spatial, non-temporal referent that is revealed in space and time yet is fully contained apart from it. On the contrary, he will find that the world itself is overflowing with the searching forward of the divine presence, a commitment in line with Whitehead's sense that "that religion will conquer which can render clear to popular understanding some eternal greatness incarnate in the passage of temporal fact."[3]

Secondly, Bernard Lee will go beyond the question of the Jesus of history to ask that we understand church in a thoroughly historical fashion as well. Thus he will amplify the social critique that emerges from the Whiteheadian school, by which process theology scans the social order that classical theism has given to the story of Western Christianity, particularly its ecclesiological structure, and finds it to mirror the social failures of Western society in general. As process theology is committed to observing the effects that happen in the world, its treatment of church structures, in Bernard Lee's hands, meant that the notion of ecclesiology could never be dissociated from the struggle for wider forms of community. With the sensibility of a radical empiricist, his theological *modus operandi* was to scan the world in its overflowing busyness, attempt to see it in all its primal beauty, and throw himself in.

Whitehead's own references to the earliest strands of Christianity sound, in the abstract, fairly romantic, in his notion that the Galilean peasantry was one of "a gracious, simple mode of life, combined with a fortunate ignorance" that gave rise to humanity's "most precious instrument of progress – the impracticable ethics of Christianity."[4] In this he is quite like liberal Christianity, searching the story of Jesus and those gathered around him for the particulars of an historical moment, but airbrushing that moment even as they insist that their claims are the result of a rigorous attention to cultural context.[5] This will remain a struggle for Christian theologians, who bring an historical critique to the claims implicit in current ecclesial structures, but who also bring a vision to that critique, one which prizes some forms of community over others.

Whiteheadian thought in the hands of Bernard Lee, therefore, grounds two emphases: 1. An insistence on the facts of the matter, thus his engagement with the origins of the Christian movement, both in terms of Jesus as a Jew and the structure of the early followers of Jesus as a critique, and 2. a close attention to how social structures function to produce community, particularly as these have shaped and could shape Christian community, both in terms of formal ecclesiology and in terms of the faith-filled dynamics of small intentional groups.

But Bernard also seems to prize a third element, a largeness of spirit, which he drew from the work of Bernard Loomer on "size."[6] In this, he valued the notion of charisma as the spark of invitation and the binding force for engaged communities. This spark, this notion of size, relates, I think, to the ongoing search in process thought for an account of how novelty enters into human lives. Given that this system values the real facts on the ground of history, yet also seeks to bend that arc toward a spirit of inclusive community that is not yet concrete, there will need to be an account, in some way, that permits the entrance of novelty into the world. What is it about the "sparkers," the "in-spirited" of some Christian communities that serves in a special way to draw others in? Why does a given group of people seem different, seem to have something special? How can it be that I am drawn to a particular group, and see in their company the possibility of new way life for myself, one that seems to open up possibilities that I have never before entertained?

The interplay of these three elements also animate the questions of feminist theology, indeed, several feminist theologians situate themselves in the pragmatic school in the spirit of Dewey and Pierce. With Lee, feminist theologians are deeply committed to a historical reading of Christianity, for feminists, this would be one that gets the facts right by including women in that history. They are also committed to living Christian community in a new way that will rethink earlier social structures, particularly as these served to reinforce gender stereotypes. And with third wave critiques, the definition of those social structures, both in their critical lens for the past and in their contemporary ecclesial practice, broadened to include other persons marginalized in that history: women and men and children who were not counted due to their race or ethnicity, their gender or sexuality, their physical or mental ability.

But what also needs to be accounted for, in this scenario of emancipation, is the novelty of its vision. Where does this socially progressive story come from, how does its critique break through the prevailing social norms in a way that is persuasive? How does new life enter the world, changing who we are and for what we hope? How does a hope that is completely marginalized at one point take hold with sufficient force that it becomes reasonable and even normative just a few years later? How did that hope – foolish, fragmented, irresponsible, "crazy" – appear in the first place? How do we get an Elizabeth Johnson, who retrieves Irenaeus in our own day by arguing that the goal of feminist theology is the flourishing of women, particularly "women and their dependent children," recognizing, as she does that the flourishing of those women is part-and-parcel with that of those children?[7] Where do so many women of color find the energy and vision and depth of thought to engage the culture over and over, pointing out the blindness of privilege? How does this vision, with its critique of all that is valued by Western culture – power, masculinity, wealth, whiteness, "father-right and father-might"—come to be not just a concern, but now an accepted (though barely enacted) ethical norm?[8]

This novelty is at least in part due to the broad appropriation of process theology's critique of classical theism, if not an embrace of the entirety of process theology's treatment of the doctrine of God. (Notice that the term "novelty" doesn't only mean "brand new," as these social questions about liberation find forerunners throughout history.) Process thought eschews the sovereign – subject, dominating parent-obedient child metaphor of God-world relations for one that is more intelligible to modern science, but also (red flag) palatable for contemporary western sensibilities. God doesn't order, God asks, God cajoles. The modern reader of Feuerbach has, of course a few questions for this model. Just as the contemporary feminist wonders why, at the very minute we gave women full membership in the fully autonomous subject club we suddenly realized that fully autonomous subjects were a chimera, we also do have to be self-critical about the softly therapeutic model of God posed by liberal thought at mid-century. In other words, "novel" doesn't mean "right." But it does mean new, in the sense that Lee seeks an emergence that is not merely an evolution.

Whatever this may be, feminist reflection on process thought is of important diagnostic value because feminists, like others writing from the margins, are acutely aware of structural inequities. Other marginalized voices will share this awareness, though I would argue that a feminist – womanist, *mujerista* – analysis is of particular value for theology, because of the way in which a gendered analysis exposes the peculiarly intimate shape of the relational structures in question.[9]

But, as feminists know well, speaking a new word is a hard thing to do. But what exactly is novelty? Is it an afterthought to be occasionally accommodated? Donald Crosby thinks not. Crosby puts forward the thesis that novelty is not an add-on to the causal process, rather, while "causality is a necessary condition for novelty...novelty is equally essential to causality." Without novelty, the causes that were wholly determined by the past would result in complete stasis. Thus causality and novelty are always already "mutually entwined...neither is prior to the other, and neither is reducible to the other."[10] In the same way, because the past becomes the (somewhat novel) present, we experience what we call time. In this universe, Crosby reminds us, time is a function of the unfolding of causal relations, it is not "a container or receptacle within which" change occurs. In this sense, time is an "expression" of cause-effect relations, relations which, as this expression is always somewhat novel, have direction, they "march on." Time is internal to the universe.

Crosby cautions that creativity, as employed by Whitehead, is not necessarily a positive or constructive attribute. Change that results in novelty is not necessarily progress; "change that results in novelty" is a descriptive term; "progress" is an evaluation of change, an evaluation that is based on culturally-constructed understandings of the good. Indeed, Crosby notes, creativity that is advantageous for one group is often accompanied by collateral damage; as the ascent of one species might well mean the obliteration of another, or the creation of one form of energy for industrial use might mean the loss of habitat in another sphere: "The perpetual productiveness of the process of nature – processes of cause and effect, the passage of time, and the emergence of novelty – is accompanied, as Whitehead observes by 'perpetual perishing.'"[11]

Such creativity can – in situations in which intelligence and a social environment lead to survival and evolutionary advantage – lead to "purposive, end-directed behavior." But note what this means: "purpose within the universe" as a potential emergent, but this does not mean that there is a "purpose of the universe as a whole." We are now rather far from even a fairly broad theism.

II. Subsidiarity, intermediary structures, resilience, novelty

Yet God remains, the kind of theism proper to our own day remains a central question, whether in <u>kataphatic</u> or <u>apophatic</u> guise. Delivering a "state of the question" lecture on Whitehead in 2011, Roland Faber observed that Whitehead, fearing that creativity would be turned into yet another thing, produced "a method of unknowing if you will…Whitehead wants us, always anew, to become creative seekers and creators of new realities and ideas in the pursuit of the art of life."[12] It is this constant de-stabilizing element in Whitehead's thought that Faber finds to be most important, as Whitehead sets down a method that will priorize the aesthetic as a metaphysically creative force, emerging in novelty.

This destabilizing approach has been a theme for Catherine Keller, as a theologian but increasingly as a theorist and critic of social and political structures. Commenting on the work of William Connolly's political philosophy of "immanent naturalism," she sees there an affinity with Whitehead, observing that, for both, "[c]ausality is not then an external determinism but an enfolded influence."[13] In this, "theism" is best approached through a kind of triune apophasis, similar to the "unknowing" of Nicolas of Cusa's *docta ignorantia*.[14]

This re-reading of theism springs from and forms our understanding of human community, in which ambiguity and flux are more obviously the order of the day. The relation between theism and social forms has been a theme for trinitarian theologian and Whiteheadian Joseph Bracken. Responding to Niklas Luhmann's well-known work on social systems, Bracken argues for a subjectivity that flourishes throughout these systems, lending a dynamism – and some level of ambiguity – to the system. Bracken keeps the focus on how that subjectivity becomes a systemic element, so that systems are more than "an aggregate of constituents," as Whitehead can seem to suggest. This flexibility with the locus of subjectivit(ies) in open-ended systems derives, I argue, from Bracken's trinitarian commitments.[15]

In the light of these social commitments, and the manner in which they appropriate diverse intellectual commitments toward a common critical end, I was reminded that Bernard was a keen diagnostician of community life. His little book on community life, *Habits for the Journey*, observes that "[a]n individual's mind can get hooked into patterns. There also is something like a "community-mind," an habitual way of responding and acting. Social systems have behavioral habits."[16] With wisdom gleaned from decades of forming small Christian communities, Bernard Lee knows how to form these habits in others, what practices support this formation – and how to discuss the communal development of these practices in ways that are both supportive and self-critical.

These theoretical concerns, for which Bernard Lee showed an intensely pastoral eye, also have political and social – as Bernard would say – "cash value." For Catholic theology done in an un-critical mode, process metaphysics can seem to epitomize the threat of liberal theology, as its fundamentally open cosmos stands in direct opposition to the integralism of traditional Catholic thought, an integralism that, in recent years, problematically envelops Catholic devotional expressions as well. Yet from the sometimes totalizing tradition of catholicity comes some important lessons about structural integrity, lessons that the Church is posing – and learning – anew. One of the more "portable" ideas from the tradition of Catholic social teaching is the notion of subsidiarity, a principle that can be used in both comprehensive and open-ended systems.[17]

Simply put, subsidiarity refers to the idea that issues are best handled at the lowest level possible and the highest level necessary. In general, subsidiarity prefers the lower level, as the word "subsidiarity," refers to the deference of a higher level of authority to a level of authority that is closer to the level at which the issue functions. For example, the U.S. model of public education has long prized the local school board as the basic locus of authority for education policy. This may have some vestigial reference to the notion of the home as the first place of education, but it also links the school and the community, building on the liberal notion of an educated population for a functioning citizenry. We educate our students for our community; we shape their education to reflect our community's values.

On the other hand, the U.S. population has long been mobile, we are not simply educating our children to live in our community, we are educating them to function in a much broader culture. Thus we have state regulations for education – and state-sponsored institutions of higher education. And, given the inequities among those state standards, we end up with a national conversation around federal requirements, such as the No Child Left Behind legislation of the Bush years or the Race to the Top-Early Learning Challenge grants of the Obama administration, both of which use various federal incentives to improve struggling schools, both of which aim to prepare students for national exams such as the SAT, the gateway exam for many colleges and universities.

While these national standards are recognized, the delivery of education continues to be captive to parochialism. For example, I live in a Fairfield, Connecticut, a town with a relatively high-income population. We are directly adjacent to a large city, Bridgeport, which has a sizeable population of low-income families and over-stressed public schools. Fairfield kindergarten classes have two dozen or so students per class for the morning, with half of the class staying for an additional two hours two days a week, and Wednesday a half day for all. A five minute walk from my home places me in Bridgeport, where a kindergarten teacher handles a full class of students in the morning and a different class of students in the afternoon. Compared to a teacher in Fairfield, each of the Bridgeport teacher's two classes will have many more students for whom English is a second language (and a much broader array of first languages) and, during a single academic year, she will also cope with a much higher turnover rate. A skewed notion of subsidiarity (calls for "cohesive neighborhoods," etc.) keeps these two communities' school systems rigidly separate (and unequal), resistant to a call for a more regional approach.

Indeed, some proponents of subsidiarity, in their concern to keep their care focused on the narrowest definition of community, will turn the intellectual structure of Catholic social teaching on its head, to the point that larger structures – state or federal governments, for example – are viewed, by definition, with distrust. We see this operative in the current political climate, in which the government we choose is cast in the role of an alien force: "the government," not "our government."

The groundwork for the notion of subsidiarity appears in the foundational text for Catholic social teaching, Leo XIII's *Rerum Novarum*

(1891), though it is more thoroughly grounded in Pius IX's *Quadragesimo Anno* (1931), which indicates the need for a "more perfectly a graduated order...among the various associations"[80] The most robust account appears in John XXIII's *Mater et Magistra* (1961), which does also (to be echoed by Benedict XVI in *Caritas in Veritate*) warn about the state curtailing the freedom of individual action.

Subsidiarity is the principle that helps us to think about how institutions should properly mediate our social lives. Subsidiarity is the way in which we understand there to be structures which provide a buffer of sorts between the individual and the state, or between the individual and the whole. Subsidiarity refers to the scaffolding function of social structures and corresponding social identities. Theologically, the trinitarian notion of subsistent relations evokes the notion of subsidiarity as it keeps the many from simply collapsing in upon itself.

In the social order, intermediary institutions (for example, those celebrated by the late Robert Bellah's well-known *Habits of the Heart*) work to make life humane, by creating structures to support individuals and families, often in a manner that functions in a festive or celebratory, rather than compensatory, manner.[18] These intermediary institutions, insofar as they spill out into the community rather than walling it off, allow the community protected time and space to nurture its inner life. It is out of these structures that stronger and larger institutions will operate. Consider Bernard's push for the hard work of building consensus in community, observing that "[v]oting is the fastest, simplest and least effective way of making community decisions."[19] The work of consensus-building, however, pre-supposes intermediary institutions, as these reinforce and re-animate the relational scaffolding of the community.

Finally, subsidiarity defines catholicity in practice. If our lives are characterized by catholicity, they have both vertical and horizontal extension. Vertically, they are connected, by way of a variety of social conventions, as well as genes, with the past. Horizontally, our lives are a series of overlapping extensions. Process thought's insistence on historicity, and its thick accounting for the texture of experience, allow for the de facto subsidiarity of our commitments to be seen as the identity maker and shaper that these are. These affinities come forward, therefore, as identity producing rather than simply elective.

And these affinities build resilience. Systems that have appropriate intermediary institutions are more resilient. As a culture, we tend to see resilience as an individual factor: the ability of a single person, often a heroic figure, to respond in flexible, creative ways to stave off or mitigate unexpected disaster. But resilience can be an attribute of a community as well and this resilience derives from systemic elements, such as an appropriately targeted subsidiary structure. The principle of subsidiarity, rightly understood, is why we prefer a comprehensive plan for health insurance as opposed to a plea to neighbors taped to a coffee can by the register at the 7/11. The fact that many states have already had catastrophic-care contingency plans represents a kind of structural resilience factor, one which recognizes the structural failures of the patchwork employer-based insurance system for health care. On the other hand, as an example of institutional resilience, most large health-care facilities in the U.S. have disaster plans that address how they would bring all their resources and personnel into play in the case of a wide-spread emergency, on a regional basis. Because they know the variety of skills present in their large work-forces, they can plan to quickly convert all of their functions to emergency care. These systems demonstrate the potential resilience inherent in large organizations, insofar as each one plans to leverage its particular strengths and institutional ethos to respond to unforeseen situations.

Religious practices build resilience as well, with communal resilience built through shared rituals. We know already that our liturgical practice shapes us; less obvious is the way in which liturgy may develop our receptiveness for lively and strong institutional life. In a short essay, William van Ornum explored the parallel structure that enlivens the psalms, a practice that reinforced the message of the text and served to fix it in brains that are (perhaps) hardwired to gravitate toward this kind of structure. He reminded us of Joseph Gelineau's vivid description of how this parallelism functioned:

> The psalmist recited the verses to a simple chant, some echoes of which can be heard in certain Jewish and Christian psalmodies. These verses showed a balanced symmetry of form and sense, they scanned rhythmically in three, four, or five feet, and were linked in more or

less frequent stanzas. When he speaks a whole world of images rises from his words as they call to each other, repeating, following or clashing with each other. He makes the point not by reasoning but by hammering...[20]

Parallel structure in poetry seems at first merely to repeat a thought – consider the first verse of Psalm 19, "The heavens declare the glory of God, and the firmament proclaims his handiwork," or Psalm 15, "O Lord, who shall sojourn in your tent? Who shall dwell on your holy mountain?" But its impact goes far beyond this, functioning at a much deeper level. With parallel structure, reinforced by music or nuanced delivery, the thought comes alive, it is given rhythmic depth and metaphoric resonance. This structure gives the whole passage a tensile strength, these inner references act like rebar in concrete, bracing the structure from within but in a way that allows for some (important) vibration. Experience of this kind of ritual builds resilience at a deeply lived level.

Consider another local/regional test of subsidiarity and responsibility, drawn from the recent news. A life guard is hired by a service company to patrol a particular section of beach and coastline, its boundaries clearly marked. Someone runs up to his stand, reporting that a man is drowning in the water outside the boundary. He acts, going to the man and saving his life. He is fired by the service company for disobeying the rules; an outcry ensues against the company.

Lost in the outcry is the service company's argument: what if there had, simultaneously, been an incident in the waters he was hired to oversee? By leaving the area, the lifeguard has breached the compact: the beachgoers frolic in the water, thinking that a protective element is in place. But it is not, it has been diverted, the lifeguard is busy elsewhere. Why do we cheer this dereliction of duty? Notice that the structural element, the service company conforms to its place in the social order. Yet the lifeguard sees his charge as personal, not institutional. His most fundamental orientation is his commitment to those in danger; he – personally – has been trained to react to emergencies with a specific set of skills. On the other hand, he has been employed to use these skills for a particular set of people: those within the boundaries of the beach and marked water. In his free time, he may wander around saving anyone he wants. But during the hours of his employ, his skills are not his own, they are hired and are to be used only to protect those in the designated area.

The lifeguard's sense of agency and community prevents him from acting in the "subsidiary" capacity assigned to him. Perhaps if the service company were not so distant from the situation on the ground, this would not have come to the clash it did – principled reasons for ignoring suffering and focusing on the task at hand are more likely to be offered, and make more sense, the further away one is from the suffering. The moral use of such an omniscient distance is surely problematic, on the contrary, this case reminds us that these structures will work only if people are engaged in – enlivened by – them. And this requires a moral investment in our communities, an investment that has to happen from the outset and be tied to a specific community, of which we are a part. Our civic life, in other words, requires us to be more than "users and choosers," we first must be "makers and shapers," in order to fashion institutions that are resilient through their careful and layered use of subsidiary structure.[21]

Conclusion

To what end? All this talk of theism and institutions and community raises questions about the *telos* of the Christian project. What does it mean to assign revelatory and thus ultimate meaning to a world that is perpetually perishing? How can an open-ended society be deemed as salvific? Can we say a creed or engage in a sacramental act, knowing its inherent ambiguity – an ambiguity that Bernard Lee prized, rather than deplored – without blasphemy? We are called to live, it seems most deeply human to live, in both of these places: the world of a church whose liturgy makes ultimate claims, yet a church that is, in Christoph Schwoebel's term, "an institution of the interim." We also live with our contemporary selves that, despite our stated theological convictions, tend problematically to combine an excessive individualism with a profound suspicion of structures of authority. Properly construed, the latter may protect us. Properly construed, the former may allow for the novelty that will save us.

1   NAB Isaiah 66:14.

2   Lee, B. *The Galilean Jewishness of Jesus: Retrieving the Jewish Origins of Christianity*. NY: Paulist, 1988.

3   Whitehead, A.N. *Adventures of Ideas*. New York: Free Press, 1933, 33.

4   Whitehead, 1933, 17.

5   It is interesting to observe that both liberal and conservative theologians, while pursuing quite divergent christologies, are steadfast in their insistence on a pristine view of the life of the Holy Family.

6   Lee, B. "Loomer on Deity: A Long Night's Journey into Day," *American Journal of Theology & Philosophy* 8 (1987), 63-76.

7   Johnson, E. *SHE WHO IS: the Mystery of God in Feminist Theological Discourse*. New York, Crossroad, 2002, 150.

8   Livezey, L.G. "Women, Power, and Politics: Feminist Theology in Process Perspective," *Process Studies* 17 (1988): 67-77.

9   Howell. N., "The Promise of a Process Feminist Theory of Relations," *Process Studies* 17 (1988) 78-87.

10 Crosby, D. "Causality, Time, and Creativity: The Essential Role of Novelty," *Pluralist* 4 (2009): 47. Crosby, 2009, 54, his italics.

11 Crosby, 2009, 54, his italics.

12 Faber, R. "Three Hundred Years of Whitehead: Halfway," *Process Studies* 41 (2012): 7.

13 Keller, C. "Connolly's Mysterius Trinity Machine: A Pantheistic Reading," *Political Theology* 12 (2011), 205.

14 Keller, 2011, 207.

15 Bracken, J. "Whiteheadian Societies as Open-Ended Systems and Open-Ended Systems as Whiteheadian Societies," *Process Studies* 41 (2012) 78-80.

16 Lee, B. *Habits for the Journey: A Mystical and Political Spirituality for Small Christian Communities*. Dayton, OH: North American Center for Marianist Studies, 2000, 58.

17 Not only open-ended systems, but emergent systems also pose interesting challenges to catholicity. See Dorrien, G. "The Lure and Necessity of Process Theology," *Crosscurrents* (2008), 332.

18 For the notion of festivity, see Taylor, C. *Varieties of Religion Today: William James Revisited*. Cambridge, MA: Harvard University Press, 2003.

19 Lee, 2000, 74.

20 Cited in Gelineau, 1963, p. 5, www.americamagazine.org/blog/entry.cfm?blog_id=1&entry_id=5219

21 Cornwall, A. & Gaventa, J. "From Users and Choosers to Makers and Shapers: Repositioning Participation in Social Policy." *http://www.eldis.org/vfile/upload/1/document/0708/doc2894.pdf*

Chapter 4

God's Confronting Partners

Michael A. Cowan

> To regard God as perfect in power, as he is in vision, at the very beginning, is the most disastrous of superstitions. The "monistic superstition," as William James calls it, has worked havoc, and the most momentous decision which mankind has to make is to re-learn on that score.[1]

You are my witnesses, says the Lord. I am God (*Isaiah* 43:12). That is, when ye are my witnesses I am God, and when ye are not my witnesses I am as it were not God.

To you I lift up my eyes O you who are enthroned in the heavens (*Psalms* 123:1)... If it were not for me, i.e., if I did not lift up my eyes, Thou O God wouldst not be sitting in the heavens.

When the Israelites do God's will, They add to the power of God on high. When the Israelites do not do God's will, they, as it were, weaken the great power of God on high.[2]

A s a cradle Catholic, I spent the first thirty years of my life receiving Judaism completely through the filter of Christian theology. As I came to realize later, that was like basing my understanding of another person on what their ex-spouse says about them after a bitter divorce. Then providence struck. My good friend Bernard Lee, a distinguished Catholic theologian and my colleague in the School of Theology at St. John's University in Minnesota and later at the Institute for Ministry at Loyola University New Orleans, was among the group of scholars attempting to re-interpret Jesus by retrieving his Jewishness. That body of work is a landmark in 20th Century theology, profoundly influencing how Christians think of Jesus. When I read Bernard's *The Galileean Jewishness of Jesus*, I wept as I encountered the humanity of Jesus in a profound, unexpected way. This body of work challenged me to begin for the first time to try to receive Judaism not as "Christian Origins" but rather on its own terms, in its own right, as its own living, breathing, enduring community of faith.

In 1992 I first crossed the threshold of Touro Synagogue in New Orleans, to talk about an interracial and interfaith community organizing effort that was trying to happen in those days. In one of God's serendipitous surprises, the Jeremiah Group never realized its founders' hopes, but my relationship with Touro Synagogue became one of the spiritual treasures of my life. In my tradition there is a most fitting word for what I receive from the Touro community of faith, and that word is "grace." I grew up in the Catholic Church imagining grace as a kind of mysterious spiritual energy, like a Catholic version of what would later be called "the Force." Later I realized that "grace" comes from the Latin *"gratia,"* which means gift. And that is precisely what Touro Synagogue has been in my life.

The Talmud says, "We do not see things as they are. We see things as we are." In homage to the feisty rabbinic spirit of always adding another layer to the ever unfolding sacred conversation, I would paraphrase those wise words in this way: "We see things not just as they are, but also as we are." Human beings are interpreters. Our life experience makes possible whatever sense we can make of things, and also always limits it. So understanding well that I see Judaism not just as it is, but also as I am, I offer the following three learnings. What continues to be revelatory and compelling for me, is not only the three in themselves, but also the whole that they constitute together.

Living between two worlds

First, Judaism has given me a way of naming and embracing a tension that I have felt since my childhood. I am always troubled, and sometimes pushed to the edge of despair, by the gap between how things are supposed to be in our world and how they are. My mentor in community organizing over the past twenty years is a secular Irish-American Catholic named Edward Chambers. Ed's mentor in community organizing was an outlandish secular Jew named Saul Alinsky, who taught ordinary citizens and their leaders to recognize and draw energy to organize for change from the inevitable tension between two worlds—"the world as it is" and "the world as it should be." He taught that if we ignore the world as it should be and just tend the garden fate has given us, we lose our integrity and become passive recipients of the culture and society surrounding us. In America today, I suppose the most common form of that collective character disorder is addictive, individualistic consumerism. Alinsky also taught that if you become a fanatical purist about the world as it should be and dismiss anything short of perfection, you will drive yourself and everybody around you crazy, and be unable to organize a two-car funeral. He taught that we become as whole as we can by embracing the two-world tension and working always to move the world as it is to become more like what it should be. Such wholeness is never perfect. You work for victories, learn from defeats, take half loaves when that's all you can get, and keep on going. You do not allow the perfect to drive out the good.

For ten years, it did not occur to me that Alinsky's two worlds came from his Jewishness. Then I read the following statement in the 20th Century's best-selling introduction to religion, *The World's Religions*, by Huston Smith:

> The nature polytheisms that surrounded [ancient Judaism] all buttressed the status quo. Conditions might not be all the heart desired, but what impressed the polytheist was that they could be a lot worse.... So religion's attention was directed toward keeping things as they were. Egyptian religion repeatedly contrasted 'passionate people' to 'silent people,' extolling the latter because they didn't cause trouble. [3]

Given this religious view, Pharoah's heart may not have needed much divine hardening when the troublemaker Moses and his brother showed up at the royal doors with their outlandish demand.

> Small wonder that no nature polytheism ever spawned a principled revolution. Traditionally, Indian religion likewise had a conservative cast; for if polytheisms feared change, Hinduism considered substantive social change to be impossible.[4]

In other words, ancient Judaism's religious contemporaries believed that the world as it was, WAS the world as it should be, the only possible world, the world as the gods intended it. How convenient for the powers running the show and how devastating for those making the bricks and building the buildings. In ancient Judaism, by contrast, Smith writes,

> History is in tension between its divine possibilities and its manifest frustrations. A sharp tension exists between the ought and the is. Consequently, Judaism laid the groundwork for social protest. When things are not as they should be, change in some form is in order. The idea bore fruit. It is in the lands that have been affected by the Jewish historical perspective, one that influenced Christianity and ... Islam, that the chief thrusts for social betterment have occurred. Protected by religious sanctions, the prophets of Judah were a reforming political force which has never been surpassed and perhaps never equaled in subsequent world history.[5]

Ancient Judaism gave humanity the revelation that the social status quo we inherit is not divinely sanctioned, that what God wants is human beings committed to making our "is" look more like our "ought." Everything in the world today that goes under the name of "social justice" or "community organizing"—including America's proudest chapter so far, the Civil Rights movement—flows from the source of ancient Judaism.

> ... wherever men and women have gone to history for encouragement and inspiration in the age-long struggle for justice, they have found it more than anywhere else in the ringing proclamations of the prophets.[6]

It seems to me that in recent times we must look to Mohandas Gandhi and Martin Luther King for transformative social leadership like that of the prophets of Israel.

So a secular Jew named Saul Alinsky bequeathed to his secular Catholic protégé Ed Chambers a metaphor of two worlds that helped him name and claim the God-inspired fire in his belly in response to the gap between what was happening and what should have been happening. And Chambers passed that troubling, liberating inheritance from Judaism on to me.

God's intention for history

The second thing I have learned from Judaism is that God's intention for the world as it should be is not abstract, *laissez-faire*, or whatever we think it might be. It is quite specific. A biblical word that names God's intention for history, God's version of the world as it should be, is *"shalom."* We would have to be asleep during synagogue worship to miss how often it makes appearances in prayer, scripture and song. So, what is *shalom* with its most common English translations of "peace," "well being" and "welfare"?

A powerful statement of the centrality of *shalom* to human existence is found in the last verse of the famous letter of survival advice sent by the Prophet Jeremiah to the Jewish exiles in Babylon: "Seek the *shalom* of the city where I have sent you into exile, and pray to the Lord on its behalf, for in its *shalom* you will find your *shalom.*" Please note two things about this sentence. First, a group of people just devastated utterly by the military power of Babylon and taken away from their homeland by force, is being told to seek Babylon's welfare and pray to God for it. Imagine how that must have gone down with the survivors. Why would Jeremiah ask such a thing of his devastated people? If we accept, as I do, the assertion of my teacher Rabbi David Goldstein that "Jeremiah did not give a damn about the Babylonians," the answer is clear: "for in its well being you will find your well being" (Jeremiah 29:7) We must seek the peace of our city because without it, there is no peace for anyone. That means we cannot achieve peace alone, no matter how successful or wealthy we may be, or in a private relationship between me and God. We would do well to take these words to heart as we carry on with our lives in one of the wealthiest nations of the world so profoundly blighted by poverty.

From the perspective of Judaism, there are two great public works of peace. One is called "justice" and the other "mercy." Justice means making society's institutions function honestly, fairly, efficiently and effectively for all. Today that means seeing to it that our public schools, criminal justice systems, and city governments function well. Mercy means responding immediately to acute human need when it presents itself. That means clothing, feeding, housing and tending to the physical and mental health of our brothers and sisters who cannot take care of those things for themselves and their children. When human beings collectively practice justice and mercy to a degree and in a balance that fits our time and place, we do our part to bring *shalom* into history. Administering sanctions when mercy is called for hardens the hearts of the giver and the receiver. Bottomless mercy when people need to be held accountable destroys our moral compass, and theirs. In order to do our part of the *shalom*-making task, we have to do both, and we have to get the proportions right. How much clearer divine guidance about why we're here could we desire? What God asks is that we do our part for peace in our time and place by doing the public works of justice and mercy in the proper balance.

And just what is the proper balance? The rabbinic tradition answers, unsurprisingly, with a delightful story. Two young rabbis who have just completed their studies and are en route to their first congregations decide to ask God directly for some guidance. In their meeting with the Eternal they ask: "What would you have us do as leaders of communities of the people you have chosen?" God replies: "Have your communities look around and when they see something that calls out for justice, see that justice is done. And when they see something that calls out for mercy, see that mercy happens. Lead your communities to get the balance of justice and mercy right." The young rabbis thank God for this guidance and one of them stops on the way out with a final question: "What is the right balance of justice and mercy in the places we are going?" God replies: "Do you want me to tell you everything?" God's people must use the intelligence God gave them to arrive at practical judgments about balancing justice and mercy appropriately in their particular social locations.

Let us recall words invoked repeatedly by Dr. Martin Luther King as he led a nation toward racial peace. These are the words of Amos, "the sheepbreeder from Tekoa," who ended up in another line of work. They convey the classic warning about the spiritual risks of disconnecting the public work of worship from the public work of peace.

> I loathe, I spurn your festivals,
> I am not appeased by your solemn assemblies.
> If you offer Me burnt offerings—or your meal offerings—
> I will not accept them;
> I will pay no heed to your gift of fatlings.
> Spare me the sound of your hymns,
> And let me not hear the music of your lutes.
> But let justice well up like water,
> Righteousness like an unfailing stream.

Those who turn worship into a private experience, who let it become disconnected from our public peace-making vocation, stand in grave spiritual jeopardy. Those who fail to seek the *shalom* of the city, will not find their peace.

No community or individual gets a pass from peace-making duty. In his classic text *The Prophets*, Rabbi Abraham Joshua Heschel puts it this way: "Above all, the prophets remind us of the moral state of a people: Few are guilty, but all are responsible."[7] No one alive today created slavery, segregation or racial discrimination, but we are all responsible for interrupting the havoc that that history continues to wreak on the peace of our communities. It might help us take Rabbi Heschel's words to heart if we begin by simply recovering the root meaning of the word "responsibility," which is "to be able to respond." "All are respons-able" is a simple, declarative statement, a statement of fact. We all have the capacity to be aware of the immense social pain of our world, we can analyze what's broken there, we can organize with others of good will, and we can act together to do our limited but important part for peace. "All are responsible" is also an imperative that means "all must respond," a prophetic call to contribute faithfully to the peace of God. We all must act as agents of *shalom*.

These two learnings from Judaism have brought both strategic focus and sustaining meaning to my peacemaking work in one wonderful, wounded American city over the past twenty years.

God's confronting partners

My long encounter with Judaism has also led me to a third, jarring and liberating theological awareness. It is one that I expect to be digesting and attempting to steer my vocational course more faithfully by for the rest of my days, as I have for the past many years.

In his classic *The Varieties of Religious Experience*, William James concludes that the religious intuition of us human beings is that there is more to life that we can see, and that our well being depends on living in harmony with that more.[8] We can't see it, but must order our lives to it, if we desire peace: This is the underlying religious challenge that all human beings face, though many do not address through what is usually termed "religion." It is notable how often today people will assert strongly that they are "spiritual but not religious." Religions tell differing stories about the unseen order, and through differing rituals, teachings, and rules for community life provide ways for their members to live their lives in fidelity to those stories. Sacred stories all carry some understanding of the ultimate. The understanding of the ultimate most familiar to Westerners is, of course, God.

In attempting to describe the power of the word "God" in the lives of believers, one theologian wrote: "God is the anchor-symbol for a whole world view and way life."[9] He meant, I think, that how we imagine God profoundly affects how we see reality and choose to live our lives. The God in whom many people were raised to believe no longer anchors their world views and ways of life. They have found or are searching for other anchor-symbols. I would like to share with you a transformation of my original anchor-symbol that has been churning for many years.

Seeking the *shalom* of the world is not an isolated individual activity to be borne by human beings alone. It is a team sport, and our side of the covenant team is not alone. We have a divine partner. Taking the covenant between God and the people of God seriously—that is, taking it as a real, full-bodied relationship—means recognizing two things that clash profoundly with mainstream Christian theological tradition. First, there can be no peace without God's actions, and none without our cooperation. Second, the becoming of humans and of God are interdependent. The great Reform Jewish teacher Henry Slonimsky describes the deep mutuality between God and man in these stunning words:

> The Torah stands for goodness, for the vision and ideals and values, or the light of God in which we see light. God besides being this light and vision which we behold, is also such power, such real actual power in the universe, as is committed and has already been marshaled for the victory of the good; this power is at present still pitifully small, and that fact itself entails the drama. The power [of God] must be increased, the ideal must be translated into the real; and the active agent in this crucial event is man. ... God and man are a polarity. They are both heroes in the same drama. They need each other, they grow together but they also suffer together.[10]

This is not the God, nor the divine-human relationship, that this Catholic boy from Peoria grew up with in the 1950's, nor the one taken for granted and preached in most Christian pulpits today. That God is omniscient, omnipresent, and omnipotent, needing nothing from any creature. From that theological starting point, the notion of God needing anything from human beings is blasphemous. In addressing the omni-God in prayer and worship, many Christians to this day say: "You're God all by Yourself!" Where did this God-all-by-Himself come from?

Historians have long recognized that Christianity began in Israel, as a messianic sub-group of the Jewish community. The first Christians were Jews who believed that Jesus was the Christ, the promised Messiah. Christianity then moved very quickly, within 20 years of the death of Jesus, into the Greek cultural milieu, where its initial formal theological and institutional articulation took place. To give one critical example, the original language of all the Christian scriptures is Greek. As its theology is initially formed, Christianity takes its worldview from the Greeks. A root assertion of that worldview is captured in the maxim that "perfect being does not change." If you're trying to talk about the God of Jesus to people in the ancient Greek world, you must resort to the notion of perfection. What is perfect is fully complete, needs nothing, indeed, cannot be affected by anything. From all time it is all that it can be, all by itself. Every worldview makes possible and limits what those who dwell within it can recognize and engage. Given its root metaphor of "perfect being," the Greek symbolic matrix which gave rise to the initial formations of Christian theology had no place for a God whose power is "pitifully small," who needs human beings in order to reach fuller stature.

Slonimsky writes in the realm of religious imagination, not doctrine: "The finite God as such, of course, does not come to consciousness; he is believed in, but not formally professed. For official purposes the old omnipotent God does service. But while the one gets formal assent, the other gets real assent."[11] The Jewish midrashic imagination counters the doctrinaire mindset that forgets that all speech about God is, in the words of philosopher Alfred North Whitehead about his metaphysics, "metaphor mutely appealing for an imaginative leap." Midrash does so with images of a fully relational God emerging within a web of mutual influence, a God with partners co-emerging within that relational web with God and each other. What kind of relationship can human beings have with a perfect God who needs nothing from us and is not susceptible to our influence? The answer must be: Only a unilateral one—being influenced. Like all human interpreters, the Greek father-founders of Christianity saw things—including the God of Jesus the Jew—not just as things were, but also as they were.

In the religious world that formed me—where God is the perfect being, who by definition does not need or change—the notion that God needs humanity to realize God's intentions for history is not just strange, it shakes my foundation. And, if God is in fact the foundational symbol for worldviews and ways of life, then having our image of God transformed changes our entire existence. And that is what encountering the God whose hope for creation is *shalom*, who needs covenant partners to realize that hope, whose hands need to be untied by us, who needs us to become God as we need God to become ourselves—the God I meet in the texts and process of midrash—has done to me. That God quickens my social imagination and confirms my convictions that the web of relationships is the womb that gives birth to both peace and strife, that all real relationships are two-way streets of mutual influence, and that from such connections the becoming of all flows.

> The assertion of God in a godless world is the supreme act of religion. It is a continuing of the act of creation on the highest plane. It adds slowly to the area and substance of the Kingdom of God and to the stature of God, the translation of God as ideal and vision into the God of empirical embodiment and power. Man in whom God's creative effort had achieved a provisional pinnacle, so to speak God's own self-consciousness of his own aims, becomes from now on, God's confronting partner, and the two together a re-enforcing polarity of give and take. They become allies in the most redoubtable of all struggles and for the greatest of all stakes. They are inevitably lovers, and both of them tragic heroes. But in a very real sense the fate of God and of the future rests on the heroism of man, on what he elects to do, for he is the manifesting God and the focus of decision.[12]

Edmund Husserl insisted that all consciousness is conscious of something. Martin Heidegger described humanity as the clearing in which Being makes its appearances. Gregory Bateson suggested that in humanity the universe evolves to become conscious of itself. In the visionary passage above, Slonimsky makes human consciousness the source of divine self-awareness, of "God's own self-consciousness of his own aims." In authentic covenantal relationship, God and humanity become ever more fully aware of their respective and interrelated vocational responsibilities for bringing *shalom* to the world. In this relational process, as in all relationships, both partners are inevitably transformed.

Slonimsky also provides a link between the process/relational thought of Whitehead, which has been of such interest to Bernard Lee and through him to his students, and the rabbinic tradition.

> We come now to the boldest, most forward-reaching thought concerning God in the Midrash, to that conception of God in which the Agada anticipates the most modern speculation concerning the nature of God and his relation to man. It is this: that God depends on man for his strength and for his failure, for his growth and for his retrogression. In a world in which both are growing or in process, it is man who by his acts increases or decreases the stature of God.[13]

The testimony of Rabbi David Goldstein, Slonimsky's former student, and course notes from Slonimsky's archives confirm his view that "the most modern speculation concerning the nature of God and his relation to man" which "anticipates the boldest, most forward-reaching thought concerning God in the Midrash" includes the process/relational philosophy of Alfred North Whitehead. Whitehead's most famous theological assertion is that God's ways with the world are persuasive, not coercive. Whitehead's God influences persuasively and receives influences. It seems to me, then, that just as the philosophy of life implicit in the *midrash* prepared the beloved teacher Henry Slonimsky to receive Whitehead, the philosophy of Whitehead prepared the beloved teacher Bernard Lee to receive Judaism. And the effects of this Jewish/Christian encounter continue to ramify through history.

A final word from Slonimsky:

> God, in the full meaning of the term, is seen to stand at the end, not at the beginning. "On that day he shall be one and his name shall be one." He must be made one, and man is the agent in whose hands it is left to make or mar that supreme integration.[14]

A religious world where the full stature and integrity of the Eternal One is a work in progress and humanity plays a role in supporting or limiting the integrity, the wholeness, of God is truly another world to live in than the one into which I was born. In it, the meaning of the "God" symbol is profoundly transformed and along with it the whole world view and way of life of those who embrace a fully relational God.

So what I have learned (so far) from Judaism is, first, that through this ancient community of faith human beings first become aware that we are required to shape history according to our deepest spiritual and ethical aspirations. Second, God has a specific desire for history and its name is *shalom*; it can only come when we get serious about the public works of justice and mercy in the places where God has put us, as they are and as we are. And third, that in order to change the world and become more fully who they are, the God of history and that God's covenantal partners must join together in the peace-making process of bringing justice and mercy to time and place.

Judaism's most challenging gift to me is a more fully relational understanding of the covenant between God and God's people, and of the becoming of the parties on both sides of that partnership, than was part of my Christian inheritance. Because I cannot reconcile that gift with the God-all-by-Himself and the humanity-affected-by-but-not-affecting-God that I inherited from my tradition-of-origin, I have had to jettison those parts of my theological inheritance, to rework my anchor symbol. There is a liberating loneliness in letting that God go. The midrashic interpretation of covenant brings a new charge of ultimate meaning to my everyday acts, including my co-responsibility with God and other people for acts of peacemaking. That grace of meaning energizes and sustains my public work as a person of faith in a way that the omnipotent, already complete God does not. How important are relationships from this perspective? So important that God becomes God, human beings become human, and peace comes to history only when God and we accept our respective responsibilities as confronting covenantal partners. God is still God, and we are still human, but we stand in a relationship of real mutuality with each other. And this changes everything. In the second century of the Common Era Ireanus wrote: "The glory of God is humanity fully alive." Perhaps, nearly 1900 years later, we are prepared to imagine the related, and equally important, truth: The glory of humanity is God fully alive.

"Baruch atah, Adonai, oseh hashalom."

1   Slonimsky, Henry. "The Philosophy Implicit in the Midrash." In *Essays*. Chicago: Quadrangle Books, 1967, p. 15.

2   Midrashic commentaries on biblical texts cited by Slonimksy, op. cit., pp. 48-49.

3   Smith, Huston. *The World's Religions*. San Francisco: Harper, 1991, p. 285.

4   Ibid.

5   Ibid.

6   Smith, op. cit., p. 293.

7   Heschel, A., *The Prophets*. New York: Harper, 1962, p. 16.

8   James, W. *The Varieties of Religious Experience*.

10 Slonimsky, op. cit., p. 15.

11 Henry Slonimsky, "On Reading the Midrash," op. cit., p. 8.

12 Op. cit., pp. 31-32.

13 Op. cit., p. 48.

14 Op. cit., p. 15.

Chapter 5

The Modern Nun in the Post-Modern World

Dianne Bergant, C.S.A.

R eligious life has often been puzzling for many people, a style of living
that is quite out of the ordinary. Though its primary focus, the search
for God and for the religious meaning of life, has been embraced by
women and men down through the centuries, this search has been lived
out in many different ways. This search for God has driven individuals
like Mother Syncletica of Alexandria and Father Antony of Egypt into the
wilderness, there to wrestle with their own inner demons as well as with
the harshness of the natural elements. Despite the rigorous asceticism
of these individuals, the authenticity of their commitment to God and
the wisdom of their teaching attracted many followers. Thus religious
groups were formed, all members seeking to imbibe the spirit of their
religious mother or father and to follow an extraordinary life of prayer
and asceticism.

The Middle Ages saw an upsurge in commitment to a religious way of
life. Aflame with a commitment to God comparable to their wilderness
predecessors, men like Francis of Assisi and Dominic Guzman devoted
themselves to preaching the gospel. Not confined to monasteries, as were
the nuns and monks, followers of these men could be found in the cities,
the villages, and the countryside. Other religious groups were formed to
meet specific needs. Though many of them no longer exist, they included:
canons regular who were secular priests attached to a church and who

lived a common life; laywomen (Beguines) and laymen (Beghards) who lived for a time in community though they never took religious vows; military orders such as the Knights of Malta who defended the church through force of arms; and hospitallers who cared for those afflicted with disease.

While some women and men followed the eremitic or monastic ways of life, social restrictions usually required other women religious to remain in their cloisters, thus preventing them from membership in many of the groups founded during the Middle Ages. This significantly changed in the sixteenth century when Leo X granted permission for dedicated women to take simple vows, rather than the solemn vows that bound nuns to a particular monastery, and to engage in various works of mercy that took them out of the cloister. This led to the rise of many of the apostolic congregations that are still in existence today. Throughout the centuries, religious life has certainly taken many different forms, and each form has been a critical response to some need of the reigning culture. It is this critical stance that has consistently rendered religious life a puzzle.

A Vatican II, apostolic, woman, religious[1]

Although there are still many monastic groups of women that follow the rules of the ancient orders, the better known communities today are congregations that sprang up during the nineteenth century. Whether they are missionary foundations of foreign congregations or original North American religious institutes, members of these groups frequently consider themselves Vatican II, Apostolic, Women Religious.

Vatican II

A "Vatican II person" is one who is informed by the principles and teachings of the Second Vatican Council. And there, precisely, is the rub. By what criteria does one determine that Vatican II principles and teachings are actually operative?[2] Even before the Council was officially closed, the entire church began to experience the effects of various changes. Two words captured the nature of these changes: *aggiornamento* and *ressourcement*. The Italian *aggiornamento* means updating or modernizing; the French *ressourcement* means return to sources. While at first glance these terms might seem to be opposed to each other, the first concept meaning looking forward and the second implying looking backward, they are really complementary. They suggest that the move forward must be informed by certain values of the past.

It was not until decades after the closing of the Council that these two concepts were deliberately cast as contradictory, and this distinction seems to be growing ever more pronounced. At issue now is the way the council is interpreted. Some argue that in important matters the council did not produce anything that was radically new, but was in continuity with the teaching of the past. According to this view, it is inaccurate to speak of a pre-Vatican church or a post-Vatican church. They contend that while the Council documents contain new insights, the teachings found therein did not really veer from authoritative doctrine. Others maintain that the council promised a new beginning. No one can deny that some kind of theological development has taken place. This position, supported by the words of John XXIII, calling the Council a "new Pentecost,"[3] maintains that the council called for a radical renewal of the church.

The council documents themselves insist on their continuity with the tradition of the church. This claim is reinforced in the final report of the second extraordinary synod of bishops: "While always keeping in mind the fundamental continuity in the great tradition of the Church..." However, an exclusive emphasis on continuity is precluded in the second part of this sentence: "... interpreters must also take due account of how the council is discontinuous with previous practices, teachings, and tradition, indeed, discontinuous with previous councils."[4] It is clear that the struggle that exists between the various interpretations of the council is one of continuity verses discontinuity.

The final synodal report does provide some direction for the interpretation of the council. It states that the four major constitutions of the council, namely, *Lumen Gentium, Dei Verbum, Sacrosanctum Concilium,* and *Gaudium et Spes,* contain the interpretive lens through which the other documents should be read. However, it does not clearly identify this key. Is it their content, which has already been seen as grounded in traditional teaching? Or is it emphasis and perspective, which are very different from previous conciliar teachings? While these documents again and again appeal to church tradition, the *ressourcement* they espouse calls for a return to an early normative past, not the more recent past. It is a past that will challenge the church to engage in true *aggiornamento.* In other words, it is the emphasis of the council that is radically different, and that emphasis is unquestionably pastoral rather than doctrinal, as had been the case with previous councils. Several characteristics of the council documents underscore this difference:

> I will summarize in a simple litany some of the elements in the change in style of the church indicated by the council's vocabulary: from commands to invitations, from laws to ideals, from threats to persuasion, from coercion to conscience, from monologue to conversation, from ruling to serving, from withdrawn to integrated, from vertical and top-down to horizontal, from exclusion to inclusion, from hostility to friendship, from static to changing, from passive acceptance to active engagement, from prescriptive to principled. From defined to open-ended, from behavior-modification to conversion of heart, from dictates of law to dictates of conscience, from external conformity to joyful pursuit of holiness.[5]

It is from this new perspective that *Perfectae Caritatis* will be considered here.

The English title of *Perfectae Caritatis,* The Decree on the *Up-to-Date* Renewal of Religious Life, attests to the spirit of genuine *aggiornamento.* It calls for change, but not a complete break from the past. Throughout the document, the up-to-date renewal called for is to be accomplished in accord with the original spirit of the religious institute, thus attesting to authentic *ressourcement,* a return to the spirit or charism out of which the religious institute was born. The pastoral character of this teaching is seen in the great concern expressed for the physical and psychological dimensions of the life style, prayer, and work of the members; in the attention given to cultural, social and economic realities; and in the collaborative way in which authority is to be exercised. It is also seen in the admonition that observances and customs should be adjusted to fit the particular needs of the respective institute. The evangelical counsels are presented as ways of living out total commitment to God rather than as sacrificial renunciation, a motivation advanced in the past.

As the fiftieth anniversary of the Second Vatican Council approached, Paulist Press published a series of commentaries on the sixteen documents issued by the council. *Perfectae Caritatis* is treated in the volume entitled *Religious Life and Priesthood*.[6] After a brief history of the document is provided, its major points are discussed. These two sections are quite straightforward. It is in the description of the directives for implementation that ensuing tensions are reported.

Religious were told that renewal was to be done in light of the original spirit or charism of the institute and in light of an in-depth examination of the authentic contemporary life of the members. Each order or congregation was commissioned to identify the founding charism and to discover how the founding members were manifesting it in their present circumstances. This meant comprehensive study. The early writings of the foundresses or founders were examined, as were the political, social, and ecclesiastical circumstances of the day. It was no longer enough to know where, when, and by whom their respective institute was founded. Religious were told to discover the unique character or charism that gave it birth and meaning.

In addition to examining the founding period, they were told to trace how each successive generation understood this spirit and manifested it in its own circumstances. Once again, attention was focused on the church and society of each respective period. Hand in hand with investigation of the past went scrutiny of the present. Every aspect of contemporary religious life was probed. Members were required to examine elements of their lives, to critique and prioritize, to reaffirm or reject, to develop what was enduring or create something new. Everything that they had learned was to be questioned and reevaluated; everything that they had experienced was to be reappraised.

This was an extremely difficult task to assign to women who had spent a lifetime learning to accept and obey in silence. Communication skills had to be developed, self-confidence had to be established, and mutual trust had to be fostered within the institutes. There was considerable resistance from many who did not feel equal to the task, and unbounded anticipation from others who had felt repressed by forms of living that had been imposed upon them. A life-style that had gradually developed through a hundred years or more and to which members had been faithfully trying to commit themselves was altered almost overnight. This resulted in pain and confusion for the members and sharp criticism from many nonmembers. Hundreds were disillusioned with the entire venture and left their institutes. Much of what transpired immediately was simple adaptation. Authentic renewal would be even more arduous. Eventually the task of true renewal was viewed as a veritable refounding of the institute, a rebirth. It is very important to understand something of this critical period in the history of religious life, for it was the crucible through which most of the present-day religious passed and within which many of their values were forged.

Unquestionably, the up-to-date renewal called for by Vatican II had not been easy, but it has produced a new brand of religious. These Vatican II religious have acquired the art of communication without losing the ability to ponder and reflect. They have developed self-confidence while remaining sensitive to others. They have learned to balance assertiveness with docility, critical professional expertise with an unpretentious manner, and astounding versatility with fidelity to their original commitment.

While most religious institutes will agree that such changes were necessary, the specific manner in which change was pursued and the outcomes that followed varied from institute to institute. The character of the institute's original spirit or charism played a significant role in this diversity. However, the fundamental way in which the institute interpreted the nature of Vatican II (continuity/discontinuity) cannot be overestimated. For example, *Perfectae Caritatis* #17 states:

> The religious habit, an outward mark of consecration to God, should be simple and modest, poor and at the same time becoming. In addition it must meet the requirements of health and be suited to the circumstances of time and place and to the needs of the ministry involved. The habits of both men and women religious which do not conform to these norms must be changed.

How is this directive to be interpreted? Some focus on the phrase, "an outward mark of consecration to God," and maintain that it refers to a modified religious habit. Others point to "suited to the circumstances of time and place and to the needs of the ministry involved" to explain why they have adopted simple contemporary garb on which they attach their community's religious symbol. *Perfectae Caritatis* articulated several directives, but allowed the individual religious institutes to interpret them to fit their experience. This has generated both a plethora of diversity as well as some inevitable tension. This single example demonstrates how Vatican II religious life is often characterized by ambiguity.

Apostolic[7]

One of the most acute struggles in religious life today results from the tensions inherent in apostolic self-consciousness. Previously, religious sought to harmonize two seemingly contradictory aspects of life, the active and the contemplative. For the most part, the active life was devoted to good works and the service of others. Prayer was a necessary ingredient of this life, for it inspired and strengthened one to act with courage and dedication. The contemplative life, on the other hand, held prayer and interior union with God as primary, and everything else served that goal. Non-contemplative institutes addressed this tension by prescribing times for prayer throughout the day. Apostolic demands that took a member from this responsibility were avoided. At times members called for more periods of prayer; at other times they felt summoned to more involvement in apostolic works. Both of these aspects of religious life are valuable; both are essential. Many religious are still trying to balance them and are achieving varying degrees of success.

In the midst of the renewal inaugurated by the council, a new self-consciousness began to emerge. Delving into the documents that described their foundation and early years, religious discovered a drive that only can be called apostolic. They found that the women and men who brought their institutes into being were imbued with the same spirit as were the apostles of the early Christian era. Like the first missionaries, these apostolic-minded Christians left the warmth and security of familiar surroundings in order to bring Christ and the Gospel to those who had no one to minister to them. Instructed by Vatican II's exhortation to recapture the original charism or spirit of the institute, and inspired by the zeal of the foundresses or founders, religious were awakened to a new self-understanding. They could no longer live a modified monastic life-style; nor was it enough to increase their apostolic involvement. An entirely new worldview was developing, one that insisted that the world is not to be shunned; it is to be transformed, and religious are to be a kind of leaven in this transformation. Such a world view can only be characterized as apostolic.[8]

It is very difficult to understand what apostolic means. With so much of the world writhing in pain as it is, with children and women and men often living lives of desperation as they do, it is so easy to be overwhelmed by the needs pressing on every side and to be incapacitated by obvious limitations. One wonders if there is any use in even trying. What lasting good can come of it? How effective will limited apostolic work be? Faced with these realities, religious turned to the Scriptures with new questions. They were seeking new insights and finding new inspiration.

The early Christian tradition proclaimed that Jesus is the living manifestation of the righteousness and tenderness of God. Accordingly, a Christian is called to be a living manifestation of the righteousness and tenderness of Jesus. Furthermore an apostle is sent to bring this righteousness and tenderness into the lives of others. One might say that apostolic spirituality is the forming of Christ in the apostle; and apostolic ministry is the forming of Christ in others. The circumstances of life wherein the spirituality is developed characterize the nature of the spirituality. Apostolic spirituality is characterized by response to the circumstances of a life that is apostolic. But what does it mean to form Christ, and is there a difference between forming Christ and continuing the ministry of Christ?

What makes a life apostolic? What attitudes are essential? Was not being sent in obedience enough? Was not patient endurance of the hardships of ministry evidence of 'imitation of Christ'? These are some of the soul-searching questions that faced religious in the wake of Vatican II.

The earliest letters of the Apostle Paul insist that participation in Christ refers to a pattern of life that flows inevitably from an intimate union with that one who suffered the trials of the Messiah. The early followers of Christ were not to their view suffering solely as their entry into heaven. Their trials were to be seen as a share of the struggles of the 'final age,' the age that announced the victory of God rather than human accomplishment. Hope amid such a struggle was more than a hope for the end of suffering. It was the conviction that human weakness and sin would not prevail and that, even in the throes of adversity, righteousness would survive. This conviction often demanded blind faith and patient endurance.

Paul further insisted that the very weaknesses and limitations of the human condition provide the arenas wherein the saving power of God can be effective. He believed that the acknowledgment of human powerlessness could make room for the power of God. This is not to say that the power of God would always affect something beyond human limitations. It meant, rather, that the limitations need not determine the direction of one's life. The limitation is a limitation and remains such. Paul saw that confronted by one's limitations, one could settle into a false and sometimes sinful compensation. Paul saw that some people tend to deny their limitations and frequently run away from hardship. They often disguise their vulnerability behind masks of power and superiority, thus supporting the fiction that fulfillment is based on human accomplishment. It was against this general attitude that he spoke.

Paul's depiction of the apostolic life and the spirituality that flows from and supports it became an example for many apostolic religious. Their own apostolic life made tremendous demands on them. The acceptance of its rigors, its perplexity, and its disappointments did not take the suffering away. In the face of this suffering, they were warned against seeking less-than-Christian ways of coping. Their response could not be directed primarily by their limitations, or by the limitations of the situation. Paul's example inspired them to cling to hope. It prompted them to persevere in forming Christ in themselves and in those to whom they ministered. Their sharing in the ministry of Christ, their various forms of teaching and healing, might have appeared to be wanting and at times even futile. But they were assured that it was in the actual exercise of the ministry with all of its demands and responsibilities that Christ was being formed in them and that they would form Christ in others.

Such apostolic commitment is a formidable task for people who have been reared in a society that judges the value of an undertaking by its relative success. When obstacles appear to be insurmountable, when relationships become too demanding, when projects no longer guarantee a hundredfold, they might be encouraged to redirect their energies and to embark on ventures that promise more for less. In the face of this, the council mandated religious to take on whole-hearted, unselfish apostolic commitment.

The new apostolic self-consciousness that religious have achieved has forced them to reevaluate their ministerial commitments. If they had been founded to serve the poor and the neglected, the marginal and the forgotten, those rejected by society or beyond the reach of the church agencies, perhaps the Spirit was calling them anew to these or to similar apostolic fields. Perhaps, like the first missionaries, they too must leave the warmth and security of familiar surroundings in order to bring Christ and the Gospel to those who have no one to minister to them. For many this has meant that the operation of well-established works be handed over to others, and that the religious venture out into new fields as their foundresses and founders had done.

This move has frequently brought them into conflict with people accustomed to the former roles played by religious and resistant to new ones. It has catapulted them into social, political, and ecclesiastical arenas where, like their spiritual ancestors, they may have to contend with structures at variance with the message of the Gospel. They may be "afflicted in every way, but not crushed; perplexed, but not driven to despair; persecuted, but not forsaken; struck down, but not destroyed" (2 Corinthians 4:8-9).

How are they to cope in the midst of this tension? They are to find consolation in the conviction that they are responding to the call of God, a call that does not take them out of the world but, faithful to the summons of Vatican II, situates them at the heart of its "joy and hopes, griefs and anxieties...,"[9] there to transform it by making Christ present. Their lives witness to an alternative way of living, a way of righteousness and tenderness, a way of service and collaboration, a way that, in a selfish indulgent society, is genuinely countercultural.

The notion of community has taken on an entirely different importance for such religious. No longer is it limited to common life with varying dimensions of uniformity. Different life-situations call for different life-styles. The pressing needs of people cannot always be programmed, and so schedules vary, complicating the question of community prayer, community meetings, and community participation. Once again tensions abound. While all members may be committed to apostolic ministry, some see community as the incontestable wellspring from which flows authentic ministry. Others believe that community serves ministry in a supportive manner. This tension has not yet been resolved for all and plays its part in the present anxiety of religious life.

Most apostolic institutes are facing serious issues of membership. The years immediately following the council saw a drastic decline in numbers due to the departure of many members. Those who stayed have aged, and very few of these institutes can boast an influx of new members. As a response to this sobering demographic, some congregations have consolidated their provinces; other groups have merged to create new institutes. Still others have decided to face the grim prospect of dissolution. This reality has been variously interpreted. Those who criticized the manner in which these institutes adapted and renewed claim that they brought on their own demise through the wayward manner in which they interpreted the directives of Vatican II. Others believe that they were faithful both to Vatican II and to the charism of their foundresses or founders and perhaps have accomplished the apostolic purpose of their existence.

What shape apostolic life will eventually take is not certain. One thing seems clear. Apostolic religious are convinced of the rightness of the direction they have taken. They responded obediently to the challenge of the council. They engaged the entire membership in the renewal process. They believe that this is the work of the Spirit and, in spite of their mistakes and setbacks, they will continue on the path that lies before them.

Woman

The change in the self-consciousness of women religious began even before Vatican II was convened. Perhaps the most significant step in that direction was the establishment of the Sister Formation Conference in 1954. Until that time, many women religious embarked on their ministerial assignments without proper training. It was not uncommon for a religious to earn her undergraduate degree only after twenty years of summer courses. Though the Conference lacked the authority to compel institutes to comply with its recommendation of providing adequate training before assignment, most of them did. Many groups inaugurated a post-novitiate year of study as part of their formation program. Soon the majority of women religious possessed an undergraduate degree. In fact, several of them went on for graduate and post-graduate studies.

All of this occurred during a period of great social unrest in the United States. The "peace movement" was spreading across the country; "black power" was gaining momentum; and the women's movement" had entered a new wave. University campuses were rife with student protests. Religious were not immune to these movements, and they brought the spirit that motivated them back to their communities. There, the fervor of apostolic ideals, the dynamism of new-found self-consciousness, and the inspiration of hard-earned knowledge coalesced into an eagerness to put a new face on the religious institute to which they had dedicated their lives.

Having been told by Vatican II that they could no longer be satisfied with the traditional definitions and understandings of religious life, women religious focused their attention on their experience.[10] Trusting in the ever present Spirit of God and the integrity of their religious sisters, they set out to define themselves within the unique context of their respective institutes. They agreed from the outset that the entire congregation was to be engaged in this enterprise. It was not only the leaders who would decide on matters and then communicate their findings and decisions to the rest of the community, who in turn would docilely accept these decisions. All of the members were called upon to examine, to critique, to discuss, and then to come to consensus. In this way, members did not merely belong to the institute they had joined. Rather, they fashioned the institute of which they were now vital members.

Out of this experience has developed a self-confidence that readily rejects the slightest hint of the discrimination to which women previously had been subjected. Consciousness-raising activities such as discussion groups, workshops, and unstructured associations of support have contributed to a heightened self-awareness. Women religious have taken hold of their lives and are not willing to relinquish it.

This significant development explains why they were aghast when in 2008, the Vatican's Congregation for Institutes of Consecrated Life and Societies of Apostolic Life initiated an Apostolic Visitation whose stated goal was "to look into the quality of the life" of women religious in the United States. Since religious institutes exist under the jurisdiction of this Vatican office, the legitimacy of such a visitation was never questioned. However, they became aware that other factors were also in play. Though they had suffered a comparable decline in membership and a similar shift in ministerial involvement, men religious were not submitted to such a visitation. Furthermore, cloistered religious, whose numbers had also drastically diminished, were also exempt from the visitation. It seems that the Vatican concern was with the apostolic women religious.[11]

In the face of this pending visitation, many institutes saw this as an opportunity for them to review elements of religious life that they themselves had identified as troublesome. Such reflection reinforced the bonds of sisterhood both within each respective community and among the various institutes themselves. Consequently, they did benefit from the episode. However, the final report of the visitation was confidential and sent directly to the Vatican, thus leaving the sisters in the dark as to the evaluation of their religious life and ministry.

A second initiative directed toward the apostolic women religious of the United States was launched in 2008. The Congregation for the Doctrine of the Faith undertook a doctrinal assessment of the Leadership Conference of Women Religious (LCWR). Formerly known as the Conference of Major Superiors of Women, this organization consists of the leaders of religious institutes, not the institutes themselves. The Conference was established in 1952 as a response to a request issued by the Vatican's Congregation for Religious. Its threefold purpose is to assist members in their service of leadership, to foster dialogue and cooperation among the various institutes through their leaders, and to facilitate collaboration between and among members and other groups committed to similar societal needs.

The stated goal of the investigation was to foster "a patient and collaborative renewal of this conference of major superiors in order to provide a stronger doctrinal foundation for its many laudable initiatives and activities."[12] The assessment lists three major concerns: the doctrinal orthodoxy of the addresses given at LCWR annual assemblies; the matter of corporate dissent; and the question of radical feminism. These concerns are certainly within the purview of this Vatican office. However, the leadership of LCWR was stunned by the severity of the pronouncement.

While the leaders of LCWR recognize the authority of the Vatican office, they struggle with how it will be able to reconcile: the oversight of the content of addresses given at their conferences with issues of freedom of expression; the restriction on valid dissent with matters of academic freedom; the accusation of "feminist" disloyalty in the face of gender bias - the visitation and doctrinal assessment being two examples of it.

Religious

In 1983 the Vatican issued a document entitled *"Essential Elements in the Church's Teaching on Religious Life as Applied to Institutes Dedicated to Works of the Apostolate."* This document addresses issues such as the vows and community life as well as formation and government. The document states that some religious superiors requested norms that might help them evaluate some of the changes their institutes experienced. However, many religious saw this document as an attempt to curb the process of renewal. After all, the institutes had spent more than ten years carefully reflecting on their past experience of religious life, adapting aspects of their lives, and evaluating the results of new practices. They had worked diligently on rewriting their Constitutions, had submitted them for review to the appropriate Vatican office, and had received its approval. They now questioned whether an outside agency would have a better insight into their unique spirit and their lives than they would.

A statement that was considered problematic at the time of the issuance of the document and one that continues to trouble many religious states: "In their origins, religious institutes depend in a unique way on the hierarchy . . . each religious institute depends for authentic discernment of its founding charism on the God-given ministry of the hierarchy" (No. 41). This seems to imply that the work of the Spirit that called the institute into existence and that directed it throughout its history is subject to the evaluation of the hierarchy rather than that of the individuals and group to whom this unique spirit or charism had been given.

Historically, religious institutes were brought to birth when pressing needs were not being met by already established agencies. Charismatic women and men, aflame with zeal for the Gospel and with compassion for those in need, counted no price too great to pay in their service to the church. Regrettably, these unselfish pioneers often had to struggle against members of the hierarchy. Only after undaunted commitment, even in the face of such opposition, was approval for the existence of their institutes given. To assert, as this statement does, that in their origins institutes depended on the hierarchy is to ignore this fact of history.

Apostolic religious have never ceased reflecting upon and struggling with the essentials of religious life. Theirs is a life of consecrated devotion to God and to the establishment of God's reign on earth. In many instances, the circumstances of their ministerial involvement have determined the circumstances of their lives. They have come to share the poverty and marginality of those with whom and for whom they serve. They have docilely responded to the needs that they perceived. Recognizing the enormity of need and their own limitations, they have learned to bring their concerns to their prayer. These genuine ecclesial women manifest the love and compassion of God to a world that is so in need of tenderness. However, these are not passive women. They are not slow to champion the victims of oppression, to defend the defenseless, to speak for those who have no voice. Some of them have even paid for their commitment with their blood.[13]

Much of the spirituality that shaped the minds and hearts of religious before Vatican II was individualistic and fostered a withdrawal from the concerns of the world. Personal perfection was the primary goal of religious life and all else served that end. A form of dualism was frequently operative that pitted the spiritual against the material, the religious against the secular, the church against the world.

The Council reminded the entire church of its evangelical mission to the world. Its proper place is not over against society but in the midst of it. More than this, its task is not simply to bring divine grace to a godless world, but to discover and foster the sacred already at the heart of that world. This move has been felt deeply in the devotional and ascetical lives of women religious. They developed a more apostolic spirituality. They search for God in the midst of their work, not apart from it. Apostolic demands seem to have proliferated, and availability to others has become the virtue of the moment. Today the Scriptures nourish religious in new and profound ways. The image of Jesus tirelessly working to establish the realm of God or prophetically challenging the outdated structures of his time has become the model of their apostolic endeavors and the inspiration of their prayer.

Apostolic religious are convinced that the sacred cannot be sought apart from the world, and they are sorely aware of how often they still fail to discover its locus there. This may well be the most serious religious challenge facing them today, but they are grappling with it as they have with every challenge presented to them by renewal.

Like their predecessors in past periods of crisis, in many ways today's Vatican II, apostolic, women religious are in uncharted waters. They are being called upon to address urgent human needs that are not only social but are also religious in nature. Added to this challenge is the task of developing a theological understanding of who they are and what they are doing. They may have basic religious traditions that informed them in the past, but the expression of these traditions is not always helpful in new situations. Confident in the perception of their vocational call, yet unsure of the contemporary ramifications of that call, they turn to the broader church for collaboration in discernment and support in the directions that they take. They know that they must be steadfast without being unyielding, bold without being foolhardy, confident without being presumptuous, creative without being forgetful. In all of this they must be humble as together with the rest of the church they search for ways to respond to God.

1   Since the writer of this article is a woman religious, issues pertaining to religious life will be examined from this perspective.

2   This evaluation of Vatican II reflects the thinking of John W. O'Malley, S.J., "Vatican II: Did Anything Happen?" *Theological Studies* 67, mo.1, (Mar 2006): 3-33.

3   *Acta synodalia sacrosancti concilii oecumenici Vaticani II* (Vatican City:Typis polyglottis Vaticani, 1970), 647.

4   "The Final Report: Synod of Bishops," *Origins 15* (Dec 19, 1985): 446.

5   O'Malley, 29.

6   Maryanne Confoy, *Religious Life and Priesthood: Perfectae Caritatis, Optatam Totius, Presbyterorum Ordinis, Rediscovering Vatican II (New York: Paulist Press, 2008),* 175-271.

7   An earlier form of this section can be found in Dianne Bergant, "The Rebirth of an Apostolic Woman in *Ministerial Spirituality and Religious Life,* John M. Lozano, C.M.F et al. (Chicago: Claret Center for Resources in Spirituality, 1986), 77-80.

8   Many books and articles have appeared that chronicle and interpret this transformation. Among them are: Gerald A. Arbuckle, *From Chaos to Mission: Refounding Religious Life Formation* (Collegeville: Liturgical Press, 1996);

Joan Chittister, O.S.B., *The Fire in These Ashes: A Spirituality of Contemporary Religious Life* (Kansas City: Sheed & Ward, 1995); Nadine Foley, O.P., ed., *Journey in Faith and Fidelity: Women Reshaping Religious Life for a Renewed Church* (New York: Continuum, 1999); Mary Jo Leddy, *Reweaving Religious Life: Beyond the Liberal Model* (Mystic, CT: Twenty-Third Publications, 1990); Bernard J. Lee, S.M., *The Beating of Great Wings: A Worldly Spirituality for Active, Apostolic Communities* (Mystic, CT: Twenty-Third Publications, 2004); David L. Fleming, S.J. & Elizabeth McDonough, O.P., eds., *The Church and Consecrated Life* (St. Louis: Review for Religious, 1996); Desmond Murphy, *The Death and Rebirth of Religious Life* (Alexandria, NSW, Australia: E.J. Dywer, 1995); Diarmuid O'Murchu, M.S.C., *Consecrated Religious Life: The Changing Paradigms* (Maryknoll: Orbis Books, 2005); Diarmuid O'Murchu, *Religious Life: A Prophetic Vision* (Notre Dame: Ave Maria Press, 1991); Paul J. Philibert, O.P., ed., *Living in the Meantime: Concerning the Transformation of Religious Life* (New York: Paulist, 1994); Sandra M. Schneiders, I.H.M., *Finding the Treasure: Living Catholic Religious Life in a New Ecclesial and Cultural Context*, Religious Life in a New Millennium, vol. 1 (New York: Paulist Press, 2000); Sandra M. Schneiders, I.H.M., *Finding the Treasure: Living Catholic Religious Life in a New Ecclesial and Cultural Context*, Religious Life in a New Millennium, vol. 1 (New York: Paulist Press, 2000); Cassian J. Yuhaus, C.P., & Barbara Lawler Thomas, S.C.N., eds, *Religious Life: The challenge of Tomorrow* (New York: Paulist Press, 1994).

9   *Gaudium et Spes*, #1.

10 A book written by one of the leading figures of the council became a best seller of the time: Leon Joseph Cardinal Suenens, *The Nun on the Modern World: New Dimensions in the Modern Apostolate*, trans. Geoffrey Stevens (Westminster, MD: The Newman Press, 1962).

11 For an assessment of this visitation see Sandra M. Schneiders, I.H.M., *Prophets in Their Own Country: Women Religious Bearing Witness to the Gospel in A Troubled Church* (Maryknoll, NY: Orbis Books, 2011).

12 Statement of Cardinal William Levada, Prefect of the Congregation for the Doctrine of the Faith on the doctrinal Assessment of the LCWR.

13 Though many missionaries lost their lives, these few are some of the better known - Maura Clarke, M.M., Ita Ford, M.M., Jean Donovan, Dorothy Kazel,O.S.U, assassinated in El Salvador in 1980; Barbara Ann Muttra, Mary Joel Kolmer, Shirley Kolmer, Kathleen McGuire, and Agnes Mueller, Adorers of the Blood of Christ (A.S.C.), assassinated in Liberia in 1992; Dorothy Stang, N.D de Namur, assassinated in Brazil in 2005. In my own congregation Maureen Courtney, C.S.A., Teresa de Jesús Rosales, C.S.A., and Jenny Flor, C.S.A. elected to remain with the people during an uprising in Nicaraguan and paid with their lives in 1990 and 1995.

Chapter 6

Understanding the Marianist Charism and its Manifestations

Thomas F. Giardino, S.M.

W hen we try to describe the Marianist charism, we may find ourselves searching for words and struggling with the same dilemma that Mark Twain observed: "The difference between the almost-right word and the right word is really a large matter—it's the difference between the lightning-bug and the lightning."

The Marianist charism, if lived well, leads us to experience expansive, new possibilities for our lives and responding to the needs of our world. Yet, many of us who have surely experienced the Marianist charism often find it difficult to articulate or to help others understand it. We end up using lightning bugs to describe what we have experienced in our lives as lightning. Words fail us, in part, because a charism is not a "thing." A charism is an experience; it partakes of the mystery of the Spirit. It's like love: words and poetry approach some of love's meaning but never quite catch the whole. But when you are in love, you know it. A charism, like love, opens us to new potential and possibilities.

While it's essential that we experience the Marianist charism, it's also critical that we are able to more deeply understand and articulate it, if this reality is to continue in history. It's also essential that we understand that this intense and life-giving experience that we call Marianist charism has a source: the Holy Spirit.

Marianists have a vision or ideal about everyday life based on our Catholic and Marianist tradition that we believe contributes to the Reign of God in our time and place. Like our founders, we notice that our everyday life is a mixture of obstacles and supports for our vision—so we live "in the gap" between these two realities: our vision and current reality. Marianist founders in their time and place lived in this gap and experienced an uneasiness with the fragmentation and incompleteness that accompanied the French Revolution with all of its mixed consequences. Yet, for them and for us, in the tension of the gap, grace erupts as charism.

The context of charism for a people of faith begins with everyday life and God's interests for human flourishing in our individual and collective circumstances. The desire to understand everyday life with its big and little mysteries is common to all times and cultures. For example, the Fulani people of Mali tell this story:

HOW THE WORLD WAS CREATED FROM A DROP OF MILK

At the beginning there was a huge drop of milk.
Then Doondari came and he created the stone.
Then the stone created iron;
And iron created fire;
And fire created water;
And water created air.
Then Doondari descended the second time. And he took the five elements
And he shaped them into a human being.
But the human being was proud.
Then Doondari created blindness and blindness defeated the human.
But when blindness became too proud,
Doondari created sleep, and sleep defeated blindness;
But when sleep became too proud,
Doondari created worry, and worry defeated sleep;
But when worry became too proud,
Doondari created death, and death defeated worry.

But when death became too proud,
Doondari descended for the third time,
And he came as Gueno, the eternal one,
And Gueno defeated death.[1]

The story captures, in symbol and mystery, part of our human condition: trying to understand our everyday experiences. We find in our lives that, whether we are 25, 35, or 55, we are trying to understand blindness, trying to understand fire and water (consider the disasters of the Boston Marathon bombing or Hurricane Sandy), trying to understand pride and death, and trying to find meaning in this belief about eternal life that we hold onto, sometimes only tenuously.

In the midst of mystery, we are searching for meaning. We are yearning for something *more* in life. Just as the desire to understand the mysteries of everyday life is common to all times and cultures, so is the sense of uneasiness, incompleteness or limitation that seems part of the human condition—our Christian story names this as a consequence of "original sin." William James commented on this dynamic in religious experience more than a century ago.

From this place of unease, we find ourselves yearning or searching for *more*. St. Augustine was pointing to his own experience when he said, "You have made us for yourself, Lord, and our hearts are restless until they rest in you." Religions offer some solution or peace, some path to wholeness or fullness of life, some *more* about life. Jesus said, "I have come that they might have life, life in abundance." Buddha proposed the Eightfold Path leading to release from suffering.

The path is often experienced as a religious conversion or experience. Again, paraphrasing William James: this conversion is some event or awakening that connects me with something outside or inside me that is bigger than me, which leads to the solution or direction toward resolution of my uneasiness. We call that salvation in the Christian tradition or Nirvana in the Buddhist tradition. Time and again, I have heard lay and vowed religious in the Marianist Family use this type of language to describe their experience of a Marianist community; many call it their "vocation story."

This is the context for charism, any charism. In the Christian tradition, charism is the experience of God's manifestation of love for the world, for people who are trying to understand their experience of the mysteries not only of fire and air but of blindness (physical or spiritual) and death. Christians approach this in faith and hope, that, in fact, there is Good News in this mystery.

A founding charism

Marianist founder Chaminade had an experience of this movement, this grace, this energy of the Holy Spirit, where he made connections between his life, his dream and everyday life. These connections were not just to make him feel better after the devastation of the French Revolution, but they gave him insight, motivation and direction for social transformation. Like Chaminade, we have a strong belief that there is Good News for life even if it often seems shrouded in mystery. Like Chaminade, we have had experiences of sacred energy; we call it grace, the grace of the Holy Spirit that makes vital connections between our dreams and everyday life—not for ourselves alone, but for our church and our world. We call this experience of the Holy Spirit a *charism*, and subsequently for some it becomes a "founding charism."

The seminal scriptural text for our understanding of charism comes from Paul to the Christian community at Corinth:

> There are different kinds of spiritual gifts but the same Spirit there are different forms of service but the same Lord; there are different workings but the same God who produces all of them in everyone. To each individual the manifestation of the Sprit is given for some benefit. (*1 Corinthians* 12:4-7)

This New Testament text gives us the fundamental reference for a reality that the early Christian community experienced in its life together. Paul is speaking about a process by which God's Spirit becomes manifest or visible. We also notice the effect of the Holy Spirit in what we often call the "gifts": wisdom, understanding, counsel, knowledge, fear of the Lord, fortitude or courage (*Isaiah* 11: 2-3) and the "fruits": love, joy, peace, patient endurance, kindness, generosity, faith, mildness, and charity (*Galatians* 5:22). The Spirit uses our human capacities and gives us motivation to develop them into charisms.

We can describe a charism as a manifestation of the Holy Spirit working in and through the believer's natural ability—yet somehow more—and which is given for the sake of the building up God's community for the Reign of God in the world.

Spirituality and approach to service

Each founding charism sparks a style of spirituality and an approach to service. Because a charism is an *experience* of the Holy Spirit, in seeking to understand the Marianist charism (or any other), we need to think about how the Holy Spirit acts. Like other founders of spiritual and apostolic paths, Chaminade had an intense experience of the Holy Spirit that changed his life and ultimately led to what we now call the Marianist Family. Chaminade's experience of the Spirit came in response to pondering with Mary—Our Lady of the Pillar—about how to rebuild the Church and society after the devastation of the French Revolution.

Chaminade zeroed in on one action that changed the world: the Spirit overshadows Mary to bring forth Christ to the world. He was inspired to see the role of Mary of Nazareth, the mother of Jesus, as a lasting role in history. She brought forth in her body, formed and educated Jesus in the "Holy Family" for his mission of bringing about the Reign of God experienced as human dignity, freedom, justice, solidarity and reconciliation for all persons. Accordingly, Chaminade focused on the Incarnation as a source of the spirituality and the apostolic approach for the Marianist Family.

Chaminade never used the term "charism"; it wasn't available to him at the time in this context. The word came into this common usage only after Vatican II in whose documents it is not often used. Chaminade often used the phrase "spirit and method" to refer to what we now call "charism" and then he filled those terms with specific Marianist content.

So what does a charism do? One form of charism gives rise to a following of persons who have a similar experience as the founding person—they *identify* with the experience. They notice this reality in themselves (when they see it in action in others) and seek to live out this way of fulfilling their baptismal commitment. The charism leads to a particular manner of *experiencing God (spirituality)* and a way of *making a difference in the world (service)*. Followers or disciples usually initiate particular ways of acting and establish institutions, such as religious congregations, small faith communities, and schools that embody the central insight of the founding person for the sake of others.[2]

This was the case for the Marianist founder. Chaminade had a significant experience in Saragossa, where he spent much time praying and reading his New Testament. Certain passages, certain paragraphs, jump out at him. Imagine him, if you will, marking them with his yellow highlighter.

After the French Revolution, in the early months of 1800, he comes back to Bordeaux, rents a little room and begins to celebrate the Eucharist there. Other people, young and old, come to this oratory, and they get into conversations about the Church in France and in the rest of the world. They ask themselves questions, such as, how are we going to help bring about the Reign of God and evangelize after this time of great destruction of society and the Church? How can we bring about social transformation? Where is God in all this?

Chaminade shows his New Testament to others and notices that they have highlighted some of the same passages. Something resonates inside of them, like the strings on two different guitars. And the particular passages that Chaminade underlines have to do with Mary's role in history—salvation history—to give birth to Good News.

The Marianist founding charism is good news because it involves an experience of God and a method to make a difference in the world. In a famous retreat that Chaminade gave for the Marianist Family in 1821, he said

> ... God calls us not only to personal sanctification, but to revive the faith in France, in Europe, in the whole world, to preserve the present generation from error. What a noble, vast undertaking! What a holy and generous project! It is most appealing to a soul that seeks the glory of God and the salvation of men. And God has chosen us from among many others.

Imagine: "God has chosen **us**"—**you and me**—"to revive the faith . . . in the whole world." Once people realize this sense of call, there's no stopping us in the work they are to do in the world. Marianist spirituality is Incarnation-centered, meaning we take the world seriously because we believe that because God entered the world in a special way, as one of us, so persons in their flesh and blood and joy and grief are important; and the way God came into the world was through a woman, Mary. It involves principles and practices related to personal growth and political action. It takes discipline to be a disciple.

The Marianist charism

We understand charism in the larger experience of humankind and the Church as an experience of the Holy Spirit bringing the Good News of God's unconditional love for humankind. It happens in this fundamental search for meaning in our lives. For those in the Marianist tradition, the particular charism can be stated as succinctly as: "Missionaries of Mary" or more fully as: the experience of being formed by Mary to continue her mission of bringing forth Christ in his person and message as Good News for the world. While there are other formulations, there is a "core," as we'll discuss later, that needs to be preserved for its authenticity.

Marianists often speak of the "objective elements" or the manifestations of the charism in everyday life: faith, mission, Mary, community, and inclusivity.[3] Most of us encounter the Marianist charism through these manifestations. You might think of them as the doors through which persons enter into the field of grace that is the Marianist response to the needs of the world. And you might have noticed that different persons are attracted to different doors and enter the Marianist world in different ways.

Manifestations of the charism

How should we understand the manifestations of the charism? Some of the ways that members of the Society of Mary have described the manifestations include[4]:

- Faith of the heart. We strive to live the faith in a community, imitating Mary's response as a model of faith, and helping her in her mission. Chaminade stressed faith of the heart, which can be described as deeply rooted and convinced, thoughtful but not intellectualized, and reaching far beyond a few pious practices and transforming the structures of daily life and the basic insights of the human spirit. This emphasis corresponds very well to the search for transcendence and the need for a contemplative dimension in our lives and an identity anchored in something that is firm and worthy of stable and lasting commitment. Marianists thus stress a deep inner or interior spirit as a ground for action.

- <u>Missionary spirit or dynamism</u>. We participate in the mission of the Church and as the Church. The mission is the community entering into a covenant with Mary, to assist her in her mission to communicate the faith in Jesus Christ. Mary invites us, as she did the servants at the wedding in Cana, to listen to Jesus and to do whatever he tells us. Thus there are a variety of ministries that Marianists can be involved in to serve the mission. We are called in a special way to develop a new synthesis of faith and culture—and this implies an inculturation of the gospel that is deeper and more far-reaching in all the many cultures of our world. A pervasive *sense of mission*—being sent—is fundamental.

- <u>Alliance with Mary</u>. We are formed by Mary, our Mother, just as Jesus was formed as her son. We are her Family in the Church, and we help her in her mission of communicating the faith. Chaminade saw in her the source of a dynamism that allows us fully to take part, through our Alliance with her, in all the mysteries of her Son, especially in his saving mission. For Chaminade, devotion to Mary is quintessentially Christocentric. It develops in us a formative, community-centered way of acting in the world and fosters a missionary commitment.

- <u>Apostolic community</u>. We are a community of faith, gathered with Mary, which tightens the fraternal bonds of family and becomes present and active in the world today, within the Church and like the Church, in order to communicate faith. It is a community in which the members have real *responsibility* for the internal and external life of the community. As we say in the prologue of the Society of Mary *Rule of Life*: "Inspired by God's Spirit, Father Chaminade understood the rich creative possibilities of a Christian community for apostolic service. Such a community could bear witness of a people of saints, showing that the gospel could still be lived in all the force of its letter and spirit. A Christian community could attract others by its very way of life and raise up new Christians and new missionaries, thus giving life in turn to other communities. A community could thus become the great means to re-Christianize the world."

- Inclusivity/one great family. Chaminade sought to reproduce within the Marianist Family the variety and wealth of experience that exists within the Church as a whole. From the beginnings, Chaminade gathered men and women, vowed religious and lay people, persons coming from all socioeconomic classes—he used to speak of "one great family." This inclusivity offers us a generous and "catholic" vision for the Marianist charism. The "mixed composition" of the Society of Mary is a striking example of this inclusivity that highlights the experience of gospel brotherhood and the plurality of means and ministries for the work of formation in faith.

Marianist charism is more than community

Just as a house is more than one of its doors, the Marianist charism is more than any one of its manifestations. One problem with all matters that involve intangibles of the Spirit is the tendency to reduce them to something more manageable, to reduce our founding charism to *one* of its manifestations, usually community. I have heard many times in conversations by lay and religious members of the Marianist Family the phrase "our charism of community."

This reductive phenomenon is not uncommon. William Bausch, writing on the sacraments, illustrated the tendency by putting it this way:

> We have to overcome a long history of reductionism; that is, of reducing an encounter with God in Christ to a momentary time or isolated element. . . . Suppose someone of prosaic mind tried to get at the meaning of our [USA] national Thanksgiving Day. He worked at it

until at last he declared that the whole 'essence' of this holiday could be captured in the turkey wing. That told it all. But, of course, what a fantastic reductionism.[5]

So, while we may be in good company, we also do a disservice to those wishing to understand the Marianist charism. If, for example, we reduce our charism to community and neglect mission, we may spend so much time gathering and forget that we are also sent.

Understanding the Marianist charism as a symbol

These manifestations of faith, mission, Mary, community, and inclusivity are like pieces of a mosaic that make up the integral Marianist charismatic portrait. The "pieces" are interactive and interdependent in revealing the whole of the portrait.

You'll notice I'm mixing several metaphors—doors and houses, mosaics and portraits—that approach, but do not entirely capture, the meaning of the Marianist charism. I have found another mode of understanding that seems to help in our quest. That is: charisms usually function like symbols rather than signs. Two quotes might be useful:

> A symbol is not an object to be manipulated through mime and memory, but an environment to be inhabited . . . every symbol deals with a new discovery and every symbol is an open-ended action, not a closed-off object. By engaging in symbols, by inhabiting their environment, people discover new horizons for life, new values and motivation.[6]
>
> Symbols, being roomy, allow many different people to put them on, so to speak, in different ways. Signs do not. Signs are unambiguous because they exist to give precise information. Symbols coax one into a swamp of meaning and require one to frolic in it. . . . Signs are to symbols what infancy is to adulthood, what stem is to flower, and the flowering of maturity takes time.[7]

The Marianist charism is that kind of fertile reality: "an environment to be inhabited" wherein vowed religious, members of Marianist Lay Communities, faculty and staff in Marianist educational institutions, and others "discover new horizons for life, new values and motivation." The challenge is to keep real meaning in these characteristic symbols or manifestations of the charism without reducing them. The Marianist charism is highly symbolic, affective, more "curved" than straight-lined. This is part of its attractiveness, and also part of the difficulty in articulation. It does not easily yield to discursive language. So, a particular challenge today is to articulate an identity that gives meaning, yet has some boundaries (for example, you can usually notice ways of acting that embody the charism and those that do not), but that is still supple and not closed-off.

The variety of articulations of the Marianist charism, or any founding charism that is particularly fertile, can seem overwhelming to those seeking to understand it. Because a charism is of the Holy Spirit, no one articulation can authentically contain all of it. The truth of the charism is in our living of it. The point that Elizabeth Johnson, CSJ, made about religions, also is relevant for a founding charism:

> ...German theologian Wolfhart Pannenberg made a poignant observation: 'Religions die when their lights fail,' that is, when their teachings no longer illuminate life as it is actually lived by their adherents. In such cases, the way the Holy is encountered stalls out and does not keep pace with changing human experience. ....Only the living God who spans all times can relate to historically new circumstances as the future continuously arrives. A tradition that cannot change cannot be preserved. Where people experience God as still having something to say, the lights stay on.[8]

The core of the charism

The Marianist charism has a fertility that, so far, has stood the test of time and inspires people to act from its meanings – or, to change the metaphor – it is illuminating our everyday lives. Distinctions between the charism and the manifestations of its spirituality and apostolic approach are important to make so that we can preserve the understanding of what we might call the core of the charism: The experience of being *called by God, formed by Mary and sent on the mission of Christ* to embody the Good News in one's time and place.

The charism, of course, is only lived in and through its spirituality and apostolic approach and their manifestations of community, faith, mission, Mary, and inclusivity. With this appreciation, the creative Marianist imagination is free to respond to new times and cultures while remaining faithful to the original inspiration.

What does being "formed by Mary" look like in day-to-day life?" One way of understanding it is that it means belonging to and actively participating in a Marianist community or in a Marianist communal environment—whether that is a vowed religious community, a lay community, or an institutional environment inspired by the charism.

In practice this means that these communities or communal environments act in the way that Mary acted: as a person of faith, a person committed to the socially transforming mission of Jesus, a person who builds a family. To be *formed by Mary* involves openness to the influence of such a community and to act in ways to create such a community.

In this way we are formed. We receive for our lives, personally and collectively:

- A source of motivation: persons, stories, a tradition
- A sense of direction: amidst the myriad options in our lives
- A style of formation: a preference for communal dynamics

Aren't these gifts what we are looking for in the Marianist Family? This is what we can expect of a charism. The Marianist charism can yield these benefits if persons can notice in us the embodiment of these manifestations, individually and collectively.

Endnotes

1   Adapted from Ulli Beier, ed., *The Origin of Life & Death: African Creation Myths* (Nairobi: Heinemann Educational Books Ltd., 1966), 1.

2   This understanding or distinction regarding *spirituality* and *apostolate* is based on the 1978 Vatican document "Directives for the Mutual Relations between Bishops and Religious in the Church," # 11, which attempted to further develop the theology of charism after the concept was briefly mentioned in Vatican II documents.

The relevant article states:

"The very charism of the Founders appears as an experience of the Spirit transmitted to their disciples to be lived, safeguarded, deepened and constantly developed by them in harmony with the Body of Christ continually in the process of growth. It is for this reason that the distinctive character of various religious institutes is preserved and fostered by the Church.

This distinctive character also involves a particular style of sanctification and apostolate, which creates its particular tradition with the result that one can readily perceive its objective elements...."

What is clear in the *Marianist* experience is that the transmission of the charism to the "disciples" of the founding person happens with laity *and* vowed religious.

3   There is some discussion about—and some are dissatisfied—with trying to capture the manifestations in single-word concepts. I wrote to Eduardo Benlloch, S.M., a Marianist studies expert, about this and he responded: "... I think it is impossible to find a very short and precise expression. It will always require a proper explanation.... What matters most is not the name we give to these points; but rather the way we explain them, which always needs to be done. We can always come to a formula that summarizes the spirituality of the whole Marianist Family. This one, for example:

Lay, religious and priests

With a deep interior spirit

Gathered in missionary communities

In alliance with Mary

For service of the Church.

Raymond Fitz, S.M., has recently stated the manifestations this way: Formed in Faith, Nurtured in Community, Diversity United in Common Mission, Motivated by a Missionary Spirit, and animated by the Spirit of Mary.

4   This description of the manifestations of the charism is based on the recent writings of David Fleming, S.M. (Circulars 1 & 7) and Manuel Cortés, S.M., the present Superior General (*The Charism and Spirituality of the Marianist Family*). For a full elaboration of these manifestations there are many works to consult, such as the *Commentary on the Rule of Life of the Society of Mary.*

5   William Bausch, *A New Look at the Sacraments* (Mystic, CT: Twenty-Third Publications, 1983), 6-7.

6   Nathan Mitchell, "Symbols Are Actions, Not Objects," *Living Worship* 13:2 (February 1977): 1-2.

7   Aidan Kavanagh, *Elements of Rite* (New York: Pueblo Publishing Co., 1982), 5.

8   Elizabeth A. Johnson, *Quest for the Living God: Mapping Frontiers in the Theology of God* (New York: Continuum, 2007), 23.

Chapter 7

Liturgy for Life

Andrew Simon Sleeman, O.S.B.

Introduction

B ernard Lee begins his introduction to *Alternative Futures for Worship* with a story from his time in Berkeley[1]:

> *A group of friends met for Eucharist and a pot luck supper. Someone proposed a fantasy exercise. A $10 million prize was to be made available for the best dream that would enable religion to make a difference in today's world.*
>
> *They broke into groups and each group had to come up with a plan. Bernard's group won!*
>
> *This was his dream: thirty nine people, from varying professions (liturgists, sacramental theologians, historians, scripture scholars, sociologists, psychologists, novelists, two devils, three saints, two clowns, two poets, etc.) were to live together in community, for an indefinite period of time.*
>
> *Their task was to work, pray, play, fight, sing, dance, eat and drink together while exploring how contemporary people could worship in a way that makes a difference. The form of worship they proposed must help transform the world and they may not leave until the job is completed!*

My life has become a search for a form of worship that could "transform the world." This search has taken place mainly within the confines of a monastic community. I joined the Benedictine Community in Glenstal Abbey in 1970. I have come to feel more at home in this place and that is a surprise.

Part 1

My mother was a convert to Catholicism from the Church of Scotland and my father an English Catholic. We moved to Ireland when I was five. This was Ireland in the 1950's, a time when Catholicism was part of the very air we breathed. We all believed the same things about God, the Church, Jesus and the sacraments. There was heaven and hell and purgatory, a universe in three tiers and we settled for this model of reality and lived out of it.

The Catholic faith or "the faith" as it was better known, was handed on like a family heirloom from one generation to the next. The emphasis was on duty and on the rational and moral basis of "the faith." It was centered on the person of Jesus Christ and our task, as young Catholics was to imitate Him. He was our model. God the Father watched over us, a distant, fearful figure. The Holy Spirit was never mentioned except as a ghost, the "Holy Ghost" and seemed to behave accordingly.

We never questioned this faith. The great truths were revealed and we had to learn them and believe them. The learning was easy as these truths were set out neatly in a soft backed, green, Penny Catechism. It had all the answers and the pope couldn't make a mistake.

This "faith saturated culture" seeped into my consciousness and gave me a paradigm from which to live my life. Religious practice was focused on the Mass. We participated by proxy; we watched and listened and if serving mass, worried in case we got the rubrics wrong.

We compensated for the distance we felt at official liturgy by clinging to our own private devotions: brown scapulars, miraculous medals and rosary beads. Some of these devotions had special guarantees, so many souls would be released from purgatory if you said x number of prayers.

In this paradigm there was never even a hint that my inner world mattered unless of course it deviated from the religious norms. Everything we were taught focused on the outer world. We learnt about God, about the rivers of Europe, the Battle of the Boyne, triangles, the adventures of Julius Caesar, reproduction in earthworms, while the dynamics of our inner worlds were ignored, dismissed as vague, fuzzy, and unreliable. The interior life was for professional religious, those following a life of perfection and far too dangerous a place for the ordinary believer. We got devotions to keep us occupied, under control and out there.

My body was the real enemy, the site and source of my sinfulness. Its impulses could not to be trusted. Yet I knew that this was precisely where I experienced my most intense reality. Expression through bodily activity in sport and dance was where I felt most myself.

I left school in 1969. These early beliefs quickly slipped away and I began the search for a new paradigm of life. It was the 1960's and I, like most in my generation, was swept up in the dramatic changes happening all round us. Beatlemania had hit the planet and the "Fab Four" had gone to India in search of a religious teacher. All we wanted to do was to go to San Francisco and wear flowers in our hair. Even the church was changing. With the beginning of Vatican II, "timeless" certainties evaporated before our very eyes. Suddenly we were eating meat on Fridays.

I left Ireland in search of a wider canvas for my life and volunteered for work in Belize. It was paradise. I met wonderful people and my natural tendency to be physically engaged in the world was almost too much. At the end of the year I left Belize, unenlightened, and wandered through North America until it was time to go home. The question still lingered. 'What could I do to find a meaningful life'?

I remember the moment when this became clear. I was standing in the courtyard at Glenstal Abbey and felt a warm surge of energy rise up through my feet. I knew this was an invitation - my chance to find "it"- even though I had no idea what "it" was. I accepted the nudge and applied to join the monastic community at Glenstal.

Monastic life presented a new set of challenges. It was all about "surrendering," "letting go." There was even a German word for it, *Gelassenheit*. I tried to do this but failed. My inner world, untouched by the daily monastic and liturgical round, did not go away. I tried to ignore its demands by burying myself in work. I did not succeed and my body eventually forced me to stop.

It was then that I was introduced to D.H. Lawrence and read his works voraciously. He seemed to understand. He knew about the underworld and instead of ignoring it, he urged me to make a "great swerve" in my life and get in touch with my primal roots, sealed beneath the membrane that had grown across my diaphragm.

Despite this insight, a part of me still yearned for a life of order and control – wanted to quieten the messy underworld with its indecipherable tunes and strangely coded messages. But I was being nudged to move on and "guided along the right path" and I knew I had to say "yes" to the process. I clung to the lines of Psalm 115: "I trusted even when I said: 'I am sorely afflicted.'"

I went to study theology in St. John's Abbey, Collegeville, Minnesota, USA. It was 1982. I met Bernard Lee and Michael Cowan. Bernard taught me theology and Michael introduced me to the world of psychotherapy.

I struggled in therapy. The words I needed to access my inner world were not available. I tried finger painting and this allowed another form of truth to emerge - images, symbols, hints from my underworld appeared on paper. Emotions, feelings, opaque to my familiar, rational mind were finding a way out into the light. My fingers knew and the *Digitus Dei* was guiding me.

Could therapy be the answer? It was about this time that I suddenly recognized that I was not interested in the spiritual or liturgical life at all. What I was after was peace, relaxation rather than spiritual growth or liberation. Relaxing in a saline solution, in a California flotation tank, while listening to Bach, was where I was at. But I knew that therapy, though helpful, was not the final chapter of my story.

A book by Michel Tournier, *Friday or the Other Island,* based on the story of Robinson Crusoe, prompted me to study indigenous cultures.[2] In this telling of the story, Friday with his deep, organic connection with the earth becomes the hero. I envied his relationship with the earth. I visited indigenous peoples and found that their life and particularly their rituals had a vibrancy foreign to me. I bought their commercially produced art cleverly on sale in airports. I have a dream catcher above my bed and a piece of aboriginal art hanging in my office. I soon recognized that this attempt to adopt the spirituality of another culture was a false trail. This approach wouldn't take root. It was no use trying to wrap myself in the tempting and exotic spirituality of another culture. I had to face the poverty of my own soul.

Part 2

I am the monastery's beekeeper and in 2005, I was ambushed going to work with my bees! Abbot Mark Patrick Hederman O.S.B. and Dr. Noirin Ni Riain were planning to run a course in Glenstal called, "Liturgy and Life." They were proposing liturgy as a source of life and wanted me to teach part of the course. I was reluctant to get involved as I knew that my life was sourced in other areas. Liturgy was part of the price I paid for living comfortably in the monastery. If I prayed, I preferred to do it on my own, through yoga and meditation. And my bees provided me with a rootedness and a contact with the natural world.

But somehow I knew this was another invitation. And I was at a point in my life when sports and other activities were becoming increasingly unrealistic as sources of life. It was time to try and understand liturgy and adjust to this complex and, for me, unnatural way of relating to God.

Most people who write about liturgy attempt to explain what happens at the other side of the tapestry where Christ is sitting at the right hand of the Father surrounded by choirs of angels and saints. I struggled with this approach and lacked the capacity to understand what happens in this dimension. I needed to find some spiritual, emotional, and psychological "pitons" that could help me understand how liturgy could be a source of life. A piton is a metal spike (usually steel) that is driven into a crack or a seam in the rock with a hammer, and which acts as an anchor to protect the climber against a fall or to assist progress. These are my pitons.

1. A workable definition of liturgy

During the first year of the course, I came across several definitions of liturgy: The "work of the people," the "ontological activity" of the Church, "the summit of the Church's activity," and "the source of its sanctification." This was abstract stuff. I understood the words but struggled to find in them any sort of reality. And I still wasn't convinced that I needed to do any more than my private prayer to detect the inner tappings of the Holy Spirit guiding me to life.

One definition stood out - liturgy as something we "do," rather than something we think about, an "-urgy," like metallurgy rather than an "-ology" like psychology. It is the technology we use to make a connection with the divine, with the mystery. The idea of mystery needed clarification.

2. Mystery as "a problem to be solved"

My rational, scientific bias meant I approached "mystery" as a problem to be solved. And if I couldn't solve it, I walked away paralysed by my incapacity to understand it.

Fr. Gregory Collins, author of *Meeting Christ in His Mysteries*, and also part of the Liturgy and Life team, made it clear that in order for the church to survive, it had to come up with some 'new and creative ways into the mystery', rather than trying to simplify or dilute it in a vain attempt to reengage the disenchanted.[3]

Raniero Cantalamessa suggests that rather than trying to explain or run away from mystery, it is more effective to bathe in it, submerge in it, love it and feast at its table.

> One cannot take in the ocean but one can do something better, allow oneself to be taken in by it, submerging oneself anywhere in its expanse. This is what occurs with Christ's passion. The mind cannot wholly take it in, nor can its depths be seen but we can submerge ourselves in some moment of its reoccurrence.[4]

That was a helpful image. But if I was to bathe in it, there had to be an ocean dense enough to support me but not too dense or frozen to prevent the mystery unfolding.

Bathing implied the participation of the imagination – the "central organ of theology" and one of the organs dismissed during my education as "vague, fuzzy and unreliable." Without it I would miss out on "what is coming from elsewhere;" miss out on "the very tremulous and delicate vibrations on the ether which represent our connection with God."

3. Grappling with symbols

Establishing "new and creative ways into mystery" depends on the use of effective symbols. I am more comfortable dealing with "fact and reason" rather than with metaphor or symbol. And this despite the learning during therapy, that metaphor and symbol give access to another kind of truth.

If liturgy is to become a source of life, it is vital to relearn the language of symbolism, the language of the mysteries of Christ. It means dislodging my dominant rational consciousness, and releasing a self that is naturally celebratory, cosmic and capable of ecstatic experience. It means diving below layers of sophistication and refinement and reconnecting with the so called "primitive" or mythic layers of my psyche, those which operate symbolically and engage the sacred.

Some images have helped me to understand how symbols work. One was to view them as portholes to the invisible. Another was to see them as walls which separate but also connect like prisoners who communicate by knocking on the wall between them. The wall separates but also connects. Liturgy is both a barrier and a "way through" to the "other" world.

But the most helpful image for me was the placenta. The placenta is a temporary organ which holds two blood networks close together, close enough to allow the exchange of materials but with no direct connection. This disjunction is necessary as the pressure of the mother's blood is too powerful for the delicate blood vessels of the developing embryo. Liturgy acts like the placenta, using symbols as a temporary symbolic organ to bring us right up against the invisible world so we can receive the energy of divine life without being overpowered.

Michelangelo's painting of the creation scene in the Sistine Chapel also provides another striking image. Here the life-giving finger of God reaches out and almost, but not quite, touches the outstretched finger of Adam. Effective liturgy is how we bridge this gap. It does so by weaving a delicate tracery between the fingertips of the human and the divine.

4. Liturgical consciousness: Praise, blessing and thanksgiving

If liturgy is the technology of contact then praise is what we use to connect the fingertips of the human and the divine. Praise is a natural activity for human beings and situates me in the most appropriate relation to my creator. It helps to steer a course between the loneliness and alienation of my conquering rational consciousness, which constantly seeks to impose an ideology on the world and the idolatry of attempted fusion with Mother Earth in some blissfully unconscious form of Edenic oneness. This "liturgical consciousness," achieved by embedding a "liturgy of praise" in my daily life, offers a middle way.

Walter Brueggeman describes this unique attitude of liturgical co-creation as "doxology," meaning the right way to give praise, of "willingly yielding" as unconditional surrendering (*Gelassenheit* again!). This is the alternative to tightening up and being defensive as I try to create a new pivot point for my life. This willingly yielding, this evacuation of ego, this growing awareness of being guided, is hugely challenging, particularly for those of us who grew up believing we were in charge of our world!

5. The Secret Agent

The Holy Spirit is at the heart of liturgy. For most of my life the Holy Spirit has been presented as a ghost and behaved accordingly. Any yet we proclaim in the Creed, "I believe in the Holy Ghost, the Lord the giver of Life."

Part of our problem is how to conceptualize this Spirit. The early church had no such difficulties, they used images portraying it as a dove. Celtic Christians, however, imagined it as a wild goose, a very different, less comfortable type of bird. A goose is a belly bird, constantly making noise, honking and attacking anyone who tries to contain it. That sounds more like the inspired prophets of old. We tend to neutralize this spirit, turned it into something sweet, sentimental and dove-like. We are no doves. And I suspect the spirit isn't either.

The Holy Spirit is the dynamic force at the centre of the liturgy, the transmitter of divine life to the world. It is crucial that we establish new ways of relating to her or else we end up with a liturgy and a life that is inert and lacking in adventure. Effective liturgy is one way of allowing the Spirit to become a powerful, transforming agent at the heart of our lives.

6. 'Breakthrough to the mystical'

Karl Rahner stated unambiguously that the "*The Christian of the future will be a mystic or will not exist at all.*" And I am sure he is right. We have to …. "*recover what was understood so well in the early centuries of the church's life that the celebration of the liturgy….. is the objective point of entry into genuine Christian mysticism.*[5] People don't want to know "about" God but want an experience "of" God. They want a breakthrough to God.

There is a poem which describes a man constantly searching for something. One day he is asked what he is looking for. "*I'm searching for God*", he said. "*And please don't tell me I'll find him in my heart, (though in a sense that is true). And don't tell me I'll find him in my neighbor (although in a sense that is true too). What I am looking for is a God making a five sense breakthrough to humanity.*" The goal of liturgy is to provide such a breakthrough, such an entry point into the mystical. We don't need to go to India, or further east. Catholicism already contains a rich mystical tradition and its sacramental system could and should link us with the heart of this spiritual experience.

But liturgy is not solely about re-connecting to a deeper and more profound presence. It is not solely about generating altered states of consciousness or providing an ecstatic experience. Liturgy is also about making a difference in the world, it is about having our hearts enlarged and releasing an unrestricted love. Liturgy, as a "creative way into the mystery," will enrich people's lives so that they have the energy and the love, to reach out to the other. Liturgy must help cultivate the inner, mystical life which complements, rather than replaces, the church's traditional emphasis on social justice.

7. Hinge of salvation

Tertullian states that our bodies are the 'hinges of our salvation.' More recently, Kunzler points out that even the recent "*liturgical reform ….is afflicted by its "enmity towards the body"......the liturgy must "win back its character as event, as an activity expressed in gestures and symbol, in short its character as a fully human act. Do we trust our liturgies any more to provide us with the ecstasy of belief?"*[6]

If liturgy is to become a way into the mystical, and provide us with access to the ecstasy of belief, then it must engage the body and the senses more effectively. It is easy to understand why this is so. We are still hard wired to nature and have not somehow managed to jettison this part of ourselves in favour of our rational minds. Our so called primitive nature is still very much part of who we are.

The church, at least in Ireland, is singularly out of sync with society in understanding the crucial role of the body and senses in ritual. For example, fasting, at one time a mark of Catholic identity, was abandoned after Vatican II but is now all the fashion as people recognize its health benefits.

Chant, once the preserve of the church, has vanished from most liturgy yet secular chant courses are widely available as people understand intuitively the benefits of this type of singing. There is a monastery in France which introduced the vernacular after Vatican II. After a while the monks became depressed. A consultant was hired to find out what had gone wrong. He recommended that they reintroduce chant – they did so and the depression lifted!

In some churches candles have been replaced with electric lights to switch on as you make your donation. And yet in many homes, candles are an integral part of family gatherings. Incense too, is more likely to be found in people's homes than in churches. People know instinctively that the senses must be engaged for affective ritual.

Liturgies are overly cerebral and many of the prayers continue to echo a negative view of the body, sexuality and the feminine, while nature, too, is continually devalued. This is a strange aberration given that the church insists on using natural elements such as ashes, water, beeswax and oil.

The hosts we use as communion wafers in most parishes are symbolic of this attitude. They are meant to be bread, but since matter is evil, as much of it as possible must be removed, so this "bread" becomes the bread of angels (*panis angelicus*) and can melt on my tongue. To maintain their purity, these wafers of immateriality were, at one time, baked by clerics wearing surplices.

Engaging the body in general and senses in particular, requires more than simply kneeling, standing or simple body awareness. Engaging the senses, through the use of colour (vestments), smell (incense) sound (chant) etc. is vital if liturgy is to provide an affective, effective five sense breakthrough in people's lives. Engaging the body through processions or liturgical dance offers other ways this could happen.

8. Readiness for ritual

One further element seems essential if liturgy is to be transformative, adequate preparation. Prior to Vatican II, significant time and energy was given to fasting and dressing with great care. These days we tend to simply show up and expect the liturgy to work.

A first step must be to slow down our noisy, busy minds, striving to achieve something. The narthex in the church was at one time a space to help participants move from their busy outer world into a more receptive state of consciousness. In most churches, it is now simply an entrance porch where you are asked to turn off your cell phone.

During the "Liturgy and Life" course we introduced a "narthex experience" to help participants step out of their busy lives and to tune into the delicate sacred. They gathered in the Icon Chapel, a small chapel under the main church. Participants took it in turns to set up the space and lead the gathering in quiet reflection. From this transition space, the participants moved to the main church for Sunday Eucharist.

Conclusion

Over the last forty years I have searched for a way of life that was energizing and true. My search has moved in many directions and seems to be settling on the possibility of living 'liturgically,' embedding in my day an underlying scaffolding of praise and thanksgiving. This is a surprise.

Somehow I have found the beginnings of a link between my internal life and the life of liturgical worship. It as if I have drilled a bore hole and have finally broken through to an under layer from where praise and thanksgiving rise up through me naturally as a spiralling energy.

What has happened is like the "miracle" that happened to Helen Keller. Helen who was a blind, deaf and dumb was taught to finger spell by Anne Sullivan. She poured water over one of Helen's hands while she spelled out the word water with her finger on the other hand. Something about this movement and contact helped to explain the meaning of "the word" to Helen and she finally understood. Helen recalls this incident in her autobiography: "I felt a misty consciousness as of something forgotten, a thrill returning thought and somehow the mystery of language was revealed to me...."[7]

I have had many teachers, including Bernard Lee and Michael Cowan, who have helped to reveal the "language of life" to me. The *Digitus Dei* (The Holy Spirit) has spelt out the "word" on one hand while many others poured the water of life over my other hand. Something about this contact and movement has clarified the work of liturgy.

Liturgy is no longer something imposed on me or a means of escape, from "real life." It is a source of life and holds me open to participate in the co-creation of a new world. There are moments when I feel lighter, freed from the constant, oppressive activity of forging significance, each moment of every day. I can now adopt a posture which allows the "other world" to secrete itself into and become a living presence in my world.

1   Lee, B. *Alternative Futures for Worship.* Collegeville (MN): Liturgical Press, 1987, 9-10.

2   Tournier, M. *Friday or The Other Island,* Penguin, London, 1974.

3   Collins, G. *Meeting Christ in his Mysteries, A Benedictine Vision of the Spiritual life,* Columba, Dublin, 2010.

4   Cantalamessa, R. Sermon in the Vatican during Easter Week 2010.

5   Collins, G. *Meeting Christ in his Mysteries, A Benedictine Vision of the Spiritual life,* Columba, Dublin, 2010

6   Kunzler, M. *The Church's Liturgy,* Continuum, London, 2001, p. 102.

7   Keller, H. *The Story of My Life,* [1903; New York: Cosimo Inc., 2010], p.12

Chapter 8

The Life of Faith for the Life of the World

Peter Eichten

Prologue

It was a cold February night in 1983; there were tears in my eyes! I was sad, confused, and kicking myself for being an idiot. I was driving home from my first class at St. John's University in Collegeville, MN. The class was on "The Sacraments of Vocation" the instructors were Michael Cowan and Bernard Lee. I had somehow missed a reading assignment for this class and I had no idea what these guys were talking about. It was a three hour class and I was totally lost.

My wife, Jane, and I had recently made some live-changing and difficult decisions. I had just given up my position in a successful family business; we had sold or given away most everything we owned (We were taking Matthew 19:21 literally: "...sell what you possess and give to the poor...and come, follow me.") After this first class at St. John's I was kicking myself for being so stupid. The last thing I wanted was theological double-talk that had little, or nothing, to do with the real world.

I was staying with old friends who lived close to St. John's. My wife and our five small children were a hundred miles away. They were packing our belongings since we had recently sold our house, and were getting ready to move to the St. John's area. I wanted to call her and tell her the whole thing was a huge mistake, and that we needed to figure out a way to keep the house. We also needed to contact my brother and father and beg them to let me back into the family business. Fortunately, my friends convinced me not to call my wife just yet, and persuaded me to continue with the first week of schooling.

I stayed at St. John's, I went to my classes, the experience improved, and Bernard became my advisor, teacher, and good friend. Over the twenty months that I spend at St. John's, I was fortunate to have taken a total of five outstanding classes from him.

That was just the beginning of a treasured life-long relationship that I have been privileged to have with Bernard. Over the years Bernard has given me a whole set of wonderful gifts. He gave me permission to never be afraid to question important issues. And he gave me an understanding that faith has little or nothing to do with religion and has everything to do with relationships and with being engaged with the world in a meaningful way.

During my first semester I was also taking a seminar that was being taught by Bernard. I'll never forget that seminar. He asked the class, "If you believe that Jesus saves, what is it that we are being saved from?" The question was answered in many different ways from the members of the class, and I cannot remember whether we settled on an agreed upon response. It doesn't matter. What mattered was the question itself. In sixteen previous years of Catholic education, and of being active and involved in the Church all my life, I had never heard anyone ask that question. That question had never been asked before, because the answer for most of the Catholic world was obvious – Jesus saved the world! Jesus saved us from damnation, Jesus' saving action brought us to eternal salvation, or simply Jesus saved us from our sins. Bernard was suggesting something new and different here. I'm not sure I comprehended it completely at the time but it had to do more with the life and ministry of Jesus than it did about some kind of a supernatural saving power. Bernard was helping me to see that there were theological foundations behind some of the uninformed theological inklings I had as I entered St. John's. This experience had promise!

In the same class Bernard asked what the difference was between the words Jesus, Christ, and God. Was there a difference? If there was, what was it? Again, a question I'd never heard anyone ask. It was never asked because those three words were synonymous; they all meant the same thing. "No, no, no," Bernard said, they are all different, they all have very different meanings, and if we were going to be involved in the Catholic world in any meaningful capacity we needed to be able to understand and make those distinctions. I will not dwell on those distinctions as most of the contributors to this work could explain them much better than I can. I just need to say that those questions have stayed with me over the years, and have helped me ask other difficult questions about our faith.

"We are our relationships." If I had a dime for every time I heard Bernard say that, I'd be rich. The thing is, I am rich because he said it so many times, and it has become foundational for me in all the work that I do.

Understanding the importance of relationships reinforced a notion I had brewing inside of me before I came to St. John's and met Bernard. What he helped me to do was not only to understand relationship development as being important, but also to learn how to develop relationships in a particular way. That particular way is with mutuality, vulnerability, reciprocity and an integrity that is based in faith. A faith which is much more about being faithful to a God who loves unconditionally than it is about belief. A faith that is faithful to the ministry of Jesus a ministry filled with compassion, justice, and love. I have worked to carry that idea of relationship building into all that I have done and continue to do as I try to live out a life filled with faith.

An equally important gift that Bernard gave to me was an understanding that being faithful to the ministry and mission of Jesus is about being engaged in the world in a way that is trying to make a difference. The difference being attempted is to bring justice to all. My life has been spent trying to do exactly that. I must admit I have not done it very well, but it's not for a lack of trying.

But perhaps the greatest gift Bernard gave to me came from the above mentioned seminar that asked about the saving action of Jesus and the distinction between those three words, Jesus, Christ, and God. As I continued studying with Bernard at St. John's and beyond, these questions have become paramount for me. For me, these understandings are ultimately about either creating a theology that keeps people content with the status quo or creating a theology that moves people to work seriously to make the world a better place.

I didn't know it then, but Fall-Redemption Theology was being challenged when Bernard asked those questions. It is clear to me now that the saving action of Jesus deals with what is going on here on earth. It is not about some unknown afterlife. It is not about a God asking for a human sacrifice to redeem the world.

Bernard had given me another way to think and talk about Jesus, Christ, and God. He had given me a theology that was in process, it was a theology based on creation, and not on the need for "the son of God" to die on a cross. For the past twenty-five years I have been on an exciting journey about who and what Jesus of Nazareth was all about, about who this Christ figure is, and how Fall-Redemption/ Atonement theology can be replaced. It has continued to be fascinating, exciting, frustrating, and, oh, so much fun!

The journey

I was born and raised in the Catholic Church. I had eighteen plus years of Catholic education. When Jane and I were married we had three priests concelebrate the union. A year after that "over-the-top" wedding ceremony we found ourselves in the Peace Corps in Iran.

Jane and I became Peace Corps Volunteers in 1970, we taught English in Iran for two years, and loved every minute of it. Living and teaching in Iran was the most life-forming and life-changing experience of our lives. During our Peace Corps time, reading and learning became important to me for the first time in my life. As I read I began to question many of the religious concepts that I had received as a cradle Catholic.

Spending two years in a Moslem country added to the questions we had about Christianity and Catholicism. Our major concern was what the Church was doing for peace and justice in the world. When we returned home from the Peace Corps I began to research the Church's position on peace and justice. I was learning about something called Catholic Social Teaching. It was interesting that in my eighteen years of Catholic education I had never heard of Catholic Social Teaching. I had to learn about it on my own. As I read about its history and what it stood for I was greatly impressed. That research helped me to discover what was happening in Latin America and liberation theology.

Despite my strong negative reaction to the sexism in the Catholic Church, because of Catholic social teachings, liberation theology, and certain individuals, the Church was becoming an ever stronger force in my life. In the late 1970's and the early 1980's I was being greatly influenced by:

- Walter Ulrich, a retired UCC pastor from New Ulm, MN, was a constant champion for peace and justice. His untiring commitment to justice had a huge impact on me.
- Daniel Berrigan, S.J.'s influence on me had been significant, and I had the opportunity during this period to be able to pick his brain one-on-one. That gave me an insight into him that made a lasting impression on me. He was so at peace with who he was in his rock solid commitment to non-violence. A commitment that, surprisingly for me, came to him from our Catholic tradition.
- Bishop Raymond Lucker of New Ulm, MN was a friend of mine. His commitment to justice and his work to include women in the deaconate made me proud to have him as a friend.
- Bishop Raymond Hunthausen of Seattle was also an inspiration. While I did not know him personally, his commitment to peace and justice was well documented during this time and had a profound influence on me.
- Jim Wallis and the Sojourners community were also influential. Jim is an ordained minister in an evangelical denomination. He and the Sojourner community's commitment to justice continue to be about living faith in the real world.

All of these influences led me to the conclusion that the Catholic Church was a place that cared about peace and justice. So, in 1981 I sought a job in the Church, working for peace and justice. I actually had a number of interviews that went well, but always ended with the same message: "You do not have any theological training." So with the help and support of the small community to which Jane and I belonged, we made the decision to simplify our lives, and go off to St. John's to get the theological training that everyone said I needed.

This decision was the most difficult and challenging one that Jane and I had ever made. My parents were not pleased. We had just had our fifth child, and my mother was convinced that they would not only be deprived of ever having the opportunity for a college education, but might actually starve to death! My father said to me, "What is wrong with you? You are throwing away the American dream to pursue some idealistic fantasy." But, once they saw that we were serious about pursuing this "idealistic fantasy" they quickly rallied behind us and supported us every step of the way.

I entered St. John's with a chip on my shoulder. It seemed rather ridiculous to have to get "theological training" to be able to work with the Church on issues of peace and justice; nor had school ever been one of my favorite activities. (I had been in college in the middle of the Viet Nam conflict, and the only reason I stayed was to avoid the draft.) I wanted to work for peace and justice and I thought the Church would be a good place to do that. So why did I need this diploma? It was nonsense in my estimation. So, I entered St. John's in February, 1983 with the attitude that I'd get this stupid degree with a minimal amount of effort and just keep working on issues of peace and justice while going through the motions.

After the first few months in Collegeville, the chip on my shoulder was gone. I was out on the quad on Fridays protesting the presence of ROTC on the St. John's campus. I was excited learning about progressive theology, and I was developing a relationship with Bernard which made me proud to be in the School of Theology. I had found another ordained Catholic who was making sense and sharing with me the radical social nature of the ministry of Jesus of Nazareth. And he was passionate about small Christian communities. God works in mysterious ways! I went on to have the best two years of my life studying at St. John's.

Since leaving St. John's in 1984, I have spent years working for the Church in various capacities. In 1989 I became the parish administrator at St. Joan of Arc, a very progressive Catholic parish in Minneapolis. For close to twenty years it was a perfect fit for me, a parish deeply concerned about peace and justice and doing things to demonstrate that concern. However, with the conservative backlash to Vatican II, even places like St. Joan of Arc are buckling under the pressure coming from the Archdiocese and from Rome.

For thirteen of my twenty years at St. Joan's I worked with George Wertin, a brilliant, progressive pastor. George and I strove diligently together to put sacrificial/atonement theology on the shelf. In its place we tried to teach what we believed was a theology more faithful to scripture and to the life, death, and resurrection of Jesus. With George

116

leading we began to question how we worshipped, especially how we worshipped Jesus. One of the key questions was, "Can an over-emphasis on worshipping Jesus diminish what it means to follow him?" I was working with a creation-centered theology, with strong leanings toward process theology, which Bernard had introduced me to in Collegeville.

On Palm Sunday of 2000, I gave a homily explaining our version of creation-centered theology. It has had an impact that is still difficult for me to grasp. It touched people in a way that I never expected, and what I shared with those gathered for worship that day came directly from what I had learned from Bernard.

One of the many classes I took from Bernard was one on Christology. The big question that arises in Christology classes is: Is he or isn't he? Is Jesus really God or not? I came into this class with a huge bias. My self-taught theology after the Peace Corps had me questioning the Christian doctrine of the divinity of Jesus. There were two things that really bothered me about the doctrine. If Jesus was God then why didn't all people, or at least all religious people, accept that? And, when I looked at the awesome vastness and complexity of creation, it felt very arrogant to me for humans to claim that the creator of the universe was a human being. Of course, the class did not end with a definitive answer to the question about the divinity of Jesus, but it gave me some wonderful insights into the historical reality of Jesus Nazareth, as well as the connection creation has with divinity.

So, I want to share parts of that homily on Christology from a creation-centered perspective with you. The theology professed in it is almost totally a product of what I learned from Bernard. I may have taken it a bit farther than he would. I dare to share this years later only because of the responses it received; to this day I continue to receive requests from parishioners of St. Joan's to share this homily with them.

The context: It was Palm Sunday, but we did not read the Passion; instead we chose Matthew 21: 1-11, known as "The Triumphant Entry into Jerusalem."

Here is the text of my sermon:

> How do you see Jesus? From the gospel today it would be
> easy to see Jesus as King, as Lord, as Master, as a great
> hero, with a triumphant entry into Jerusalem. I'm not

going to break open this story today, other than to say it cannot be taken literally, and Matthew's intention of this story is satire. The Kingly way is being mocked. Jesus' ministry was in direct opposition to being King, Lord or Master. And yet for many of us today understanding Jesus as King, as Lord, as Master is very much a part of our Christian belief system.

What I do want to break open today is why that is true. Why is understanding Jesus as King, Lord, Master and God the prevalent way of seeing Jesus in the Christian world? And I want to investigate if there is there another way of understanding Jesus.

I will attempt to do this by talking a little bit about Christology. Christology is the study of Christ, or how we understand Christ. In over simplified terms, there are in our Christian tradition 2 kinds of Christology; what we can name as a high Christology or Christology from above and what we can name as a low Christology or Christology from below.

You see, a funny thing happened on the way to Christianity: the one who came proclaiming, became the proclaimed one! Jesus of Nazareth, a Jewish peasant came proclaiming the Reign of God. He came proclaiming a particular way of being in the world. He came proclaiming a way that would break down the hierarchy of his day. He came proclaiming a way that was about the equality of all people regardless of sex, national origin, or birth right. He came proclaiming a social ministry that was based on compassion, justice, and love. But, early in the Christian tradition, it became more important to worship Jesus than to follow Jesus. The social message of Jesus became submerged, and worshipping him as God became paramount. How did this happen?

Christological understandings give us a clue as to how this came about. A high Christology begins with understanding Jesus as God. That understanding causes other theological ramifications. The most obvious is why did God have to become human? So, a whole theology was developed to answer that question. In a very simplified way it goes something like this: There is something inherently evil with the world; and, therefore there is something inherently evil with being human. (The Christian doctrine of original sin most clearly states this.) So, the world and humanity need to be redeemed from this inherent evil. To do this God had to become human to save the world. This is known as fall/redemption, sacrificial or atonement theology. Most Christian denominations including Catholic churches operate out of this fall/redemption/sacrificial/atonement theology. It is a theology that is created by a high Christology. Jesus came to atone for our sins, he was sacrificed, and through the sacrifice of his life we are saved. Jesus saved us by his death, and let us praise and worship the Lord that he did that for us wretched sinners!!

There is another way to understand Jesus, an understanding from a low Christology perspective. It begins with understanding Jesus as being totally human. With a low Christology a completely different theology emerges. When you start with Jesus' humanity what emerges is a theology based in creation, a theology that affirms the goodness of creation, and the goodness of being human. Then what becomes important is not worshipping Jesus but rather following Jesus, and being human like Jesus. It's his ministry that becomes the focus, not his redeeming death. A creation-centered theology understands all of creation to be good, and that we are partners with the divine in continuing the creative process.

A low Christology and a creation-centered theology are not concerned with redemption. Jesus came proclaiming the Reign of God here and now, and putting forth a way of being in the world that is for here and now. Jesus comes proclaiming that we are loved totally by God; there's nothing we can do to be saved, God's love saves us. What Jesus made clear to us, is that we are called to respond to God's saving love. That response for us today as people of privilege comes with a huge responsibility. Jesus' ministry of compassion, justice, and love is not about some reward in an afterlife, it's about making the world right now the best that it can be for all of creation.

So to answer my beginning question, we tend to see Jesus as King, a triumphant figure, because of high Christology. And a high Christology leads to a theology of fall and redemption, a theology that concentrates on the death of Jesus as saving us, and this tends to lead us to put emphasis on worshipping Jesus as divine Savior. A low Christology on the other hand, leads to a creation-centered theology that concentrates on the goodness of being human and the goodness of creation, and this leads to following Jesus.

St. Joan of Arc parish operates out of a low Christology, a creation-centered theology, and a concentration on following Jesus. That's why social justice is so much a part of St. Joan's culture. So, perhaps the theology of our parish is a bit different from many other Christian places, and yet it is rooted squarely within our Christian and Catholic tradition, it's just that it's been on the margins.

Try to see Jesus first as a human being with the same human struggles that you have. Try to see the palms that you take with you today as a symbol of the ministry of Jesus, not the majesty of Jesus. Concentrate on the ministry of Jesus. It's about his compassion for all, his ceaseless work for justice, and his love for creation. All of this so deeply touched the lives of his early followers that they began to talk about him as being divine. I believe that our tradition also talks about that divinity in all of us and in all of creation.

Unfortunately, with the advent of the "New Roman Missal" in the Catholic Church, even a place as progressive as St. Joan of Arc in

Minneapolis is buckling under the pressure coming from the hierarchy and reverting back to an atonement high Christology.

I continue to this day to work for the Church's biblical ideal of peace through justice and mercy; however, I find it very difficult to participate in the institutional Catholic Church. I have a difficult time seeing much Christianity being lived out in the institutional Catholic Church. While many Catholics profess that they can remain in the Catholic Church by ignoring or challenging the institution and the hierarchy, I cannot. One of the main reasons I cannot is the influence that John Rawls' philosophy of justice has had on me. Simply put, Rawls stresses the importance of just institutions for a just society. While justice is clearly more than simply creating just institutions, institutions play a significant role in creating and maintaining justice. In my opinion, the institution of the Catholic Church at this time in history is corrupt. There may be some nuggets of justice coming from the hierarchy at times, but the foundation is rotten to the core. The institution's position on women and homosexuality has eroded its credibility. It is a power hungry institution that cares much more for the well being of the institution that it does for the message of Jesus.

Another path of discipleship

"We are our relationships, so the quality of our relationships matters." I heard Bernard say that more than once! When I met Bernard he was a proponent of small Christian communities. This mutual love and concern for small communities has been one of the bonds that have made our relationship special.

My hope for small communities has always been, like Bernard's, that they can be a vehicle for transforming the world. But as the multi-year national research project led by Bernard has shown, the fact is small communities of Anglos in the United States are far better at being places of care, safety, faith sharing and prayer than they are at being a transformative force in the public life.[1] The inner life of small communities may be more transformative than we have thought. Putting prayer, love, and care into the universe cannot be a bad thing, and may be more powerful than we can ever imagine. However, the socially transformative power of the small community movement remains dormant for the most part.

My personal challenge has been to try to live a life of faith that is working to create the type of world Jesus of Nazareth was trying to create: a world where love, justice, and compassion ruled. I have felt that humanizing Jesus, trying to live out of a low Christology where following him is more important than worshiping him, is a way to make the world a better place for all. And I have thought that small communities could be a place where that idea had a chance to flourish. In my thirty years in a small community that has not often been the case.

So while the small communities that Jane and I have been a part of have done some good things in reaching out, they have struggled to make an impact on issues of justice. We have been great in serving at homeless shelters, and providing in other ways the necessities for those in need. One of the reasons for the inability of our small communities to make an impact on social justice issues is the "small" in "small Christian community." Having struggled with these issues for many years, I have come to the position that in order to have a public life, to be sent as well as gathered, small communities of faith must initiate partnerships with groups and organizations working on justice issues.

In 2003 there was a severe shortage of affordable in housing in Minneapolis. As small community members it became part of our discussion but it was difficult to mobilize the entire group to any kind of action for affordable housing. Jane and I felt we could and should make a difference on this issue. I joined a task force for affordable housing created by the Twin Cities United Way, and worked on that for three years. The United Way was actually able to make a difference by working collaboratively with other local organizations working on the same issue. Then with the support of our small community Jane and I decided in 2003 to sell the suburban home where we had raised our five children and buy a duplex in the city. We would live in one unit and rent the other at an affordable cost to a low-income family. We did that, moving into one of the poorest neighborhoods in Minneapolis. This was a difficult and challenging decision, once again aided by the support and love of our small community. It has been a rewarding experience for us.

Our involvement with affordable housing was an activity that Jane and I did on our own; it was not an action of our small community. Our small community was instrumental in what Jane and I were doing with affordable housing through their prayers, support and encouragement. They were with us the whole way, but it was not a small community working in the public arena. The question remains: how do small communities engage in and with the world to make a difference? How do they become involved with justice issues and not only charity?

I am not able to answer that question. I'm not sure how to get small communities into the public arena, but I do have some inkling as to why they don't enter more readily. While I do not have empirical data similar to what Bernard collected in his national study on small communities, my experience working in parishes has given me two clues to this issue. The first is that the dominant theology of Christianity that comes from a high Christology promotes worship over working to transform the world. The second clue is that this dominant theology actually enhances American individualism because of its concentration on individual salvation.

The dominant Christian theology operative in most Christian congregations is very much centered in Fall/Redemption Theology. And it is very difficult to move people out of that theology. There is a comfort level in this theology that attracts and keeps people attached to it. It has a sense of security that is not found in the fast paced every changing society that we live in today. When this security and comfort is combined with American individualism it is easy to see how Fall/Redemption Theology continues to have a stronghold on many Christians.

I find real justice work, that is, work for transforming the world, much stronger in the broader community than it is in our Christian Churches. It is here where I find people working to end homelessness, working to end hunger, working to end war. I don't find that work very prevalent in our Christian Churches, and therefore not very prevalent in small Christian communities. Churches, and small communities, are good at charity, feeding the hungry, housing the homeless, caring for our veterans of war. In the Twin Cities Lutheran Social Services and Catholic Charities are the two largest non-profit social service agencies in the state. They do great work, but an unintended consequence of their work is that many Lutherans and Catholics in Minnesota are content to support these charities without ever asking why. While these acts of charity are needed, they don't transform the grave injustices that are prevalent in our society and in the world.

I have not abandoned my hope or my work the Church becoming a transformative agent in the world, but I have shifted my energies. I have become more active in community activities, and I have made an entrance into the world of higher education.

In 2010 I became an adjunct professor at Metropolitan State University in Minneapolis. I teach in the College of Management in the Master of Public and Nonprofit Administration program. I teach a class called "Public Ethics and the Common Good." It is a class on the importance, not only of honesty and integrity, but on the responsibility administrators in the public and nonprofit sectors have to be working for social justice.

It has been a place, in a public institution, where I have been able to share many of the concepts that I learned from Bernard. For example, I try to emulate his participatory style of teaching. I use the understandings I learned from him on relationships, collaboration, and authentic conversation. It's taken me a long time, but I finally feel that I have found a place where a difference can really be made. And it has no connection to the Church, but everything to do with faith. Once again, what I learned from Bernard about being a practical theological presence in and for the world has had a lasting impact upon my life.

In a very powerful way teaching an ethics class in a public institution has given me the opportunity to bring a low Christology to many managers and directors without ever mentioning "Jesus," "Christ," or "God." In this class social justice is presented as an ethical issue, but what is being taught is essentially the same things that Jesus of Nazareth taught.

Conclusion

If I were to give a homily on Christology today it might be a bit different than the one I gave in 2000. However, it would continue to express the concepts that I learned from Bernard: that being fully human was what Jesus ultimately accomplished, and becoming fully human is our greatest challenge. This task of striving to become fully human is done only in our relationships, so the quality of our relationships matters. "Life matters, it has consequences," Bernard says. Through all of Bernard's brilliance, his message to me is as simple as Jesus' message to all of us – becoming fully human is about being in relationships based on love, compassion, and justice. What's difficult is how that is done!

As I work in Catholic and Protestant congregations, I am often disheartened by the theological world view that many Christians hold. It is a world view based on a Christian theology that is old and outdated. It comes from our Greco-Roman philosophical tradition. Bernard has done endless work in helping Christianity recapture a more Hebraic world view; a worldview that relies not only on reason but also on the imagination; a theology that relies less on dogma and doctrine and more on valuing experience and the great depth of the human spirit.

For the years since I graduated from St. John's I have attempted to take the theological concepts given to me by Bernard and put them into a real life – mine. It has been a life-long experiment that has been rewarding, frustrating, exciting, filled with great success and great failure – it has been and continues to be wonderful!

I have changed greatly over the years. I have little patience with "God-talk." At this point in my life knowing anything about God is very precarious. Bernard taught me that we occasionally get glimpses of the Divine mainly through our relationships, and only if we are seriously paying attention. There is only one Christian doctrine that has any meaning to me anymore. It is the doctrine of grace. God's grace is there always unconditionally; there is nothing we can do to earn it or lose it. This is what I believe is at the root of the message of Jesus. It is also at the root of what Bernard gave to me – he teaches the unconditional grace of God's love, he believes it, and he lives it.

A friend of mine wrote a wonderful, but difficult song called "If Grace Is True." With his permission, I want to conclude this chapter with lyrics from that song.

> If Grace is true
> God will save you
> And all the Jews and Hitler too.
> Those with an overflowing cup,
> And those who want to blow us up.
> All little children will get in
> With those who stole their innocence.
> Who once where children just like them

And will be children once again.
But we know grace is not fair,
And that is something we can't bear.
So we take eternal truth and snuff it out
That's what we do.
Replace it with a temporal flame,
One that we control and tame.
And here's the rub though we have stayed
And say we've kept the narrow way
And keep the unclean ones away
God welcomes us in anyway.
(Hagberg, Neal, 2008 from *it's not as simple as it seems*.
Uncle Gus Music, Minneapolis)

What Bernard Lee has given me is beyond belief. My life has been enriched and made better because of his wisdom and passion. Much of what I am becoming and much of what I do is because of your influence. My gratitude for what he has given to me is endless.

1   Lee, Bernard. *The Catholic Experience of Small Christian Communities.* Mahwah, NJ: Paulist, 2000, Chapter 4.

Chapter 9

"Establish justice in the gate"

Doing practical theology after an urban disaster

Michael A. Cowan

"**P**ractical theology" has a comfortable ring to the ears of most Americans, known as we are throughout the world for our down-to-earth, pragmatic attitudes. But our usual associations to the word "practical," that is, "useful" or "applicable" or "relevant to everyday concerns," while not unrelated to its meaning in this chapter, are misleading in this instance. Rather than practical theology, we could refer to a "theology of praxis," but that would only substitute one ambiguity for another.

As Bernard Lee's writings on this subject have stressed, the hallmark of practical theology is the insistence that the point of theological interpretation is not simply to comprehend or contemplate the world as it is, but to contribute to the world's becoming what God intends that it should be, as those intentions have been interpreted by the great biblical traditions. Now the view that theology has a concrete contribution to make to the actual world might seem like common sense, but the religious instincts of many Christians have been primarily formed by the perspective of classical theism, namely, that religious experience is about knowing or contemplating the essence of things as they really are, above all, the essence of God. The difference between contemplative and transformative theologies has indeed made a difference in the history of the Christian tradition, and the title "practical theology" signals the intention to highlight the "world-making" vocation of theology.

Practical theology stresses the correlational, hermeneutical, critical and transformative character of doing theology. This is a *correlational* method because it works by holding two things in reciprocal relationship— the vision and values of our religious traditions ("the world as is should be") and the state of the actual world in which we live ("the world as it is"). It is a *hermeneutical* method because it recognizes the role of interpretation in reading our world and our traditions. It is a *critical* method because it requires that we explicitly evaluate the inherited understandings which guide our interpretations and actions. Finally, it is a *transformative* method because its constant concern is to bring the world into greater harmony with the Creator's intentions.

The method of practical theology comes down to a number of interrelated, reiterative actions. We become conscious in a troubling way of something transpiring in the world around us that should not be, or something not happening that should be. We trace the roots of our being troubled to some value that we cherish as people of biblical faith. We analyze what is causing whatever is troubling us. We return to our tradition to reflect upon what should be the case and why. We identify a feasible and faithful plan of organized action in light of our social analysis and theological reflection. We organize to carry it out. We evaluate the effects of our collective action and stay alert for the next troubling circumstances. This disciplined rhythm of reflection-action-reflection by members of a community of faith is practical theology. It is the world-making vocation to which members of communities of biblical faith are called.

Two questions about the subject of practical theology seem important as I begin. First, who does practical theology? Individuals or groups may engage in acts of mercy, but the public work of justice can only have an impact when undertaken by people acting as members of organizations and groups, including communities of biblical faith. The power of practical theology is most fully actualized when it is done, not individually, but collaboratively, by congregations, members of congregational ministry teams, small Christian communities, or faith-based community organizations acting with other civic partners, religious and secular. The subject of practical theology is not "I" but "we." The subject of practical theology is a community of faith. Social action is organized, it is collective. This is a difficult notion to grasp in an individualistic culture. The subject working to establish justice in post-Katrina New Orleans that I will describe below is a social action network, composed of religious, civic, business and government actors.

Second, what is the role of experts in doing practical theology? The faith traditions and social worlds interpreted in practical theology as a hermeneutical activity are indeed complex realities. This is indicated by the fact that scholars devote their entire lives to relatively small facets of them. For example, some scholars are experts on John's gospel, others on the theology of Augustine, others on Catholic social teaching; other specialists focus on urban poverty, criminal justice or local government. Such deep but narrow expertise cannot be required of people doing practical theology, nor is it necessary. Practitioners of practical theology need not become scripture scholars or urban sociologists, but rather must learn to read their tradition and their world—and empower others to do so—in ways that are informed by the work of experts. The goal of practical theology is not that its practitioners achieve expert status in the relevant disciplines, but that their practical wisdom—their capacity to act faithfully and effectively in the real world—be deepened by accessing what experts know in a disciplined manner. Christian discipleship, ministry and leadership must be informed by the work of experts, but not dominated by it. The point might be put in this way: Experts have their place in the work of practical theology, and must be kept in their place! Responsibility for the social analysis and theological reflection that guide and motivate doing practical theology rests finally not with isolated individuals, academic scholars or officially sanctioned leaders, but with ordinary members of communities of faith.

In what follows I will retrieve a prophetic mandate that continues to be addressed to people of faith; describe a broad and ongoing effort in doing practical theology in response to that mandate in a particular city during an extraordinary time; reflect on that effort from the perspectives of the social sciences; and close by gleaning a set of learnings about organizing to do practical theology in an urban setting.

I. Theological analysis: The biblical mandate for good public institutions

As noted above, practical theology begins when people of faith become disturbed about something transpiring in their social world that shouldn't be or something not happening that should be. For example, governmental waste and corruption, inequities in economic opportunity, and racial tensions are disturbing to people with functioning consciences. I want to begin this essay by re-reading a classic text that continues to disturb and call people of biblical faith quite pointedly and specifically to public engagement, and quite specifically to attend to the functioning of their public institutions.

The year is 760 B.C.E. A disturbed gardener called Amos goes to the central sanctuary of his nation carrying a message from their God. Standing in that sacred public space, he unleashes a barrage against the actions of the wealthy and powerful. Listen to his words.

> They hate the arbiter in the gate,
> And detest him whose plea is just.
> Assuredly,
> Because you impose a tax on the poor
> And exact from them a levy of grain,
> You have built houses of hewn stone,
> But you shall not live in them;
> You have planted delightful vineyards,
> But you shall not drink their wine.
> For I have noted how many are your crimes,
> And how countless your sins—
> You enemies of the righteous,
> You takers of bribes,
> You who subvert in the gate
> The cause of the needy.
>
> Seek good and not evil,
> That you may live,
> And so the Lord, the God of Hosts,

Will be with you, just as you have said.
Hate evil and love good,
And establish justice in the gate;
It may be the Lord, the God of Hosts,
Will be gracious to the remnant of Joseph.
(*Amos* 5: 14-15)

What is going on at the "gate" mentioned three times in this passage, and why is the speaker so upset about it? First we are told that some "hate the arbiter in the gate" and "detest him whose plea is just." Then we learn that some "subvert in the gate the cause of the needy." So at the gate, some display contempt for judges making rulings and those making just claims, and some use the procedures taking place there to take advantage of the poor. Finally, we read in the imperative mood what we are required to make happen there: "establish justice in the gate." The divine purpose of this ancient public institution is the administration of justice. What's at stake for the poor here is clear. But what are the consequences for the whole community? Only God's presence with them or absence, God's graciousness or wrath toward them.

Professor Klaus Koch offers the following description of "the gate" and what happened there.

> According to the Israelite constitution, every enclosed township has communal autonomy. In the gateway of a township of this kind—i.e., in the portico behind the one gateway in the town walls—the free, adult men of the community assembled. They alone had legal status and were empowered to take part in cultic ceremonies and to bear arms. The communal village democracy had legal and administrative competence. It decided on questions of inheritance, and even pronounced judgment in the case of capital crimes. It probably also had the task of allotting to individual members of the community the taxes or compulsory labor which the state imposed on the local community. In case of war it called up its section for the army. It looked after the local hilltop sanctuary, which its members visited. In spite of this democratic

constitution, influential families gained the upper hand, since it was they who were able to provide most members for the local council. It was a great temptation to use a majority vote to distribute taxes in such a way that families which were small and economically weak bore an undue burden.[1]

Amos and the other classic Jewish prophets first gave voice to what their secular descendant the legendary 20th Century community organizer Saul Alinsky would term the tension between *the world as it is* and *the world as it should be*.[2] Prophets speak boldly for the world as it should be when the world as it is deviates badly from God's intentions as they understand them. Huston Smith, perhaps the 20th century's most widely read interpreter of world religions argues that "Judaism laid the groundwork for social protest."[3]

When human beings fail to "establish justice in the gate," that is, create and sustain public institutions that treat all persons lawfully and fairly and without wasting limited public resources, people suffer and social peace is damaged or destroyed. For people whose sense of the world as it should be has been influenced by the ever burning vision of Amos and his prophetic counterparts of their God's intentions for history—that is, all whose world views were formed within the spheres of the historical influences of Judaism, Christianity and Islam—to "establish justice in the gate" is a fundamental social imperative. I will attempt to make the case in this chapter that unless there are good public institutions functioning at our contemporary gates, economic opportunity will be denied to those who are not insiders, damaging their life chances and those of their children in a multi-generational downward spiral. And divisive tensions among groups based on ethnicity, gender, religion and class will strengthen, limiting or destroying the peace and prosperity of the city.

For some, good public institutions are valued as matters of democracy, secular justice or fiduciary responsibility for public resources. For others, they are a religious imperative. In the hearts and minds of all who accord major importance to such institutions, the effects of the Jewish prophetic imperative to establish justice in the gate continue to reverberate. To establish justice in the gate means to create public institutions—including, but not limited to, a criminal justice system—that are lawful, fair, efficient and effective. The consequences of doing or failing to so for the poor are economic opportunity vs. scrabbling to survive. The consequences for the community as a whole are public safety and peace vs. danger and unending social conflict.

All are entitled to the benefits of the lawfulness, fairness, efficiency and effectiveness that together make public institutions good. The first of those benefits is the economic opportunity that good institutions make possible. The second is the peace that comes when inter-group trust prevails. These two common or public goods can only be enacted by citizens and public officials capable of creating and sustaining together the central public good of good public institutions. The words of Amos illuminate the religious or ultimate significance of the effort I will describe here of the people of faith who struggled together with other civic leaders and elected officials to create an Office of Inspector General to combat waste, fraud and abuse of power in New Orleans after Hurricane Katrina. In theological terms we were heeding the mandate of Amos to establish justice in the gate. The story of our effort follows.

II. Social analysis: Disaster strikes a troubled urban area, bringing challenges and opportunities

A. The storm before the storm

The last national survey of adult literacy prior to Hurricane Katrina found 40% of New Orleans adults reading at or below the 6th grade level, and another 30% at or below the 8th grade level. During the three years prior to the hurricane, New Orleanians watched as public meetings of its elected school board became models of incivility, where the politically connected struggled for control of contracts and patronage, and self-appointed activists ridiculed school officials, board members and fellow citizens attempting to raise the city's public schools out of the ranks of the nation's worst. During this same period, public officials were unable to address the deplorable condition of the city's once nationally acclaimed youth recreation department, even as homicidal youth violence escalated, putting New Orleans consistently at or near the top of national per capita murder rates.

Shortly after his election as a pro-business, reform candidate in 2002, Mayor C. Ray Nagin was denounced at a press conference of pastors by one of the city's most visible clergymen as a "white man in black skin." What had the new mayor done to so offend these powerful, politically connected clerics? He had announced that under his administration, local congregations seeking federal grants distributed through the City of New Orleans for after-school programs for children and other social ministries would be required to secure that funding by responding to public requests for proposals, and to give a formal accounting at the end of the grant period of how funds awarded were actually disbursed and with what results. A member of mayor's inner circle at the time described this public denunciation, widely reported and replayed by local media, as having had a "chilling" impact on the new, reform-minded mayor, one from which he never fully recovered.

On the evening of December 31, 2004, exactly eight months before the hurricane, a young African American visiting New Orleans to participate in a flag-football tournament was pinned on the ground by three white bouncers in a confrontation outside a French Quarter bar. Levon Jones died on Bourbon Street that night. On a cold and rainy Thursday evening some weeks later, the author chaired a public meeting in a packed City Council chambers during which the Human Relations Commission of the City of New Orleans listened for more than three hours to expressions of outrage sparked by this event and by the New Orleans Police Department's treatment of some community members over many years. Repeated predictions of impending racial riots to destroy "this plantation" once and for all were sprinkled through that testimony.

As 2005 unfolded, Katrina was not the only storm on the New Orleans horizon.

B. The immediate aftermath of Hurricane Katrina

On August 29, 2005, Hurricane Katrina grazed the mandatorily evacuated city of New Orleans, reserving its most devastating force for coastal

Mississippi just to the east. During the next two days, the federal levees protecting the city failed in multiple places. 1600 people died in the metropolitan area. Residences and businesses in 80% of the city went underwater. Public officials warned residents and business owners that they might not be able to return for 2-3 months. The scope of devastation in certain parts of the city made returning questionable indefinitely for many. Failures of coordination among local, state and federal governments added to the collective misery, and to confusion and uncertainty about the city's future.

In the aftermath, new hopes and old grievances shifted in uncertain balance, as the sense of a historic opportunity to build a better city for all vied with people's anxiety about losing whatever political and economic advantage they held before the storm. The profound disruption of local politics and economics resulting from this massive flooding created a vacuum that would both provide an opening for and provoke a contest about enhancing the well being of the whole city. For a time local civic, religious and business leaders organizing for change did not face the massive political inertia and resistance that met all such efforts before the storm. Organizing for change in New Orleans immediately after the Hurricane Katrina was like walking on the moon.

C. The Bring New Orleans Back Commission

In November of 2005, Mayor Nagin established the Bring New Orleans Back Commission, charging it to give him specific recommendations on a number of critical dimensions of the rebuilding of the city by the end of January 2006. The commission consisted of working committees of business, religious, civic and higher education leaders addressing land use, infrastructure, culture, public education, health and social services, economic development, and government effectiveness.

A local banker chaired the commission's Government Effectiveness Committee, and the author served as chief of staff. Its mission was "to ensure effective city government responses to the challenges facing post-Katrina New Orleans and to foster city government that is ethical, efficient, transparent and adequately and fairly funded." The committee's methodology was to pick key and timely targets for change; identify examples of such changes already implemented in other cities; specify the steps necessary to put such proven practices in place locally; and establish a timeline for taking those steps. The committee's stated agenda was "to build trust in city government by achieving transparency: No more deals behind closed doors."

In the temporary vacuum caused by extreme political and economic disorganization immediately following Katrina, the guiding strategic idea of committee members was that the citizens of New Orleans now had an opportunity not simply to replace what had been lost or damaged in the flood, but rather to recreate city government for the greater benefit of all by fundamentally reforming its structures, policies and operations. This initial strategic agenda was sharpened by expert adviser Steven Goldsmith's insistence that local government's principal function is to assure businesses and citizens that the city's future merits their investment. What makes businesses and citizens feel that a city's future warrants their ongoing tax dollars? Simply put, both want local government to provide its services lawfully, fairly and without waste. This is, of course, a concern of businesses and citizens everywhere.

The post-Katrina emphasis on reforming city government was further energized by the keen recognition that if local leaders were not able to alter New Orleans' legendary reputation for patronage and corruption promptly and decisively, the massive public and philanthropic funding available and necessary for the renaissance of the city could be withheld or rigidly controlled.

A review of national best practices to prevent waste, fraud and abuse provided to the committee by the Kennedy School of government suggested that an office of inspector general would be the most powerful mechanism to promote government transparency and accountability. The committee's principal researcher quickly discovered that the New Orleans city charter had mandated the establishment of an Office of Inspector General (OIG) in 1995, but an independent office had never been established. The significance of this finding was that "all" it would take to establish this key reform was a city council ordinance. Changes to the state constitution and laws or the city charter would not be required. Partly because of its strategic significance for reform, and partly because the city charter already required its establishment, the Government Effectiveness Committee prioritized establishing the OIG in its recommended "20 Steps in the Right Direction," delivered to the mayor in a plenary meeting of the Bring New Orleans Back Commission in January, 2006.

D. 2006 municipal elections

Campaigning for the first local elections for mayor and city council following Katrina set for May 2006 was beginning as the Government Effectiveness Committee made its priority recommendation to establish the OIG as a critical element of the post-Katrina change agenda. The storm's displacement of voters meant that this was to be the most highly charged election in New Orleans for many years. It included a public conversation, framed most unfortunately by the incumbent mayor, about whether New Orleans would remain a "chocolate city." A number of reform-minded city council candidates, new to New Orleans politics in the wake of Katrina, made establishment of the OIG a priority plank in their campaign platforms.

When the votes were counted, four newly elected members of the seven-member city council were fully in support of creating the OIG. The fourth was open in principle, if proper checks on the power of the office were put in place.

E. Establishing the Office of Inspector General

Making the establishment of the OIG a priority for post-Katrina reform became the basis for two significant social partnerships of government, business and civic leaders, one to establish the OIG, the other to offer it constitutional protection from politics by amending the city charter. I will describe them in sections F and G below.

After organizing the work of the Government Effectiveness Committee described above, the author founded Common Good, a group of civil society—non-profit and faith-based—organizations dedicated to seeking consensus across the lines of race, class and religion about rebuilding a New Orleans that would be better for all. Common Good began with an organizing strategy rather than a commitment to any particular issue. Since everything was broken in New Orleans after the hurricane, more issues cried out for attention than one organization could possibly address. The organizing strategy was to have a diverse group of religious and civic leaders join government and business leaders in setting priorities and implementing policies aimed at rebuilding the city for the benefit of all based on research and best national practices. In April-May of 2006, Common Good's founding leaders began by identifying issues of priority importance to them and assessing the feasibility of addressing those issues in a timely manner as a new organization. Based on that assessment, the organization's leaders chose two initial targets, public safety from violent crime and city government reform.

A multiracial, interfaith group of 15 Common Good pastors met with Mayor Nagin twice, once to offer public support for his leadership in re-building the city, and a second time to seek his commitment to support the establishment of the OIG. Common Good's executive director also met individually with business and other civic leaders to build their understanding of and support for how an effective OIG could become a powerful catalyst for moving New Orleans city government away from its legendary history of corruption and waste.

One of the newly elected city council supporters of establishing the OIG became chair of the council's Government Affairs Committee, and took the initiative in that capacity to prepare an OIG ordinance for council consideration and approval. The councilwoman and her staff sought technical assistance from the national Association of Inspectors General (AIG). That organization in turn put her team in touch with founding Miami/Dade County Inspector General. He came to New Orleans along with AIG leaders to testify before the Government Affairs Committee and brief council members and engaged citizens on best practices for establishing, funding and overseeing an ethics board and inspector general function.

In fall 2006, the city council deliberated publicly on an ordinance recommended by the Government Affairs Committee to establish an Office of Inspector General as required by city charter. It was during these deliberations that the proposed OIG was first publicly labeled a "white power grab," i.e., an attempt by whites to accomplish by ordinance what they could not do at the ballot box, namely, control black government officials. Following several hours of intense public testimony and council deliberation, the establishing ordinance was passed by the committee after adding an amendment offered by a council members providing for an oversight committee and review of the OIG's annual work plan. The whole council subsequently approved the ordinance with no other significant changes.

F. The founding inspector general

Passage of the enabling ordinance set in motion the appointment by the mayor of a seven member Ethics Review Board. Per the city charter, six of the seven appointees were chosen by the mayor from a list of nominees submitted by the city's university presidents; the seventh was nominated at the mayor's sole discretion. Following the mayor's nominations, the proposed list of founding members of the Ethics Review Board was reviewed and approved by majority votes of the Government Affairs Committee and the city council. The Ethics Review Board met for the first time in 2006. After electing a Loyola University's president, a nationally recognized scholar in ethics, as its founding chair, the board promptly initiated a national search for the city's first inspector general, ultimately selecting Robert Cerasoli, a former founding Massachusetts Inspector General from a national applicant pool.

Inspector General Cerasoli swept into New Orleans like the proverbial whirlwind. He promptly informed local media, which was keenly interested in the advent of his office and not a little skeptical of the possibility of its success, that upon refusing a city car and gas when he went to process his payroll paperwork at City Hall, he was told "But everybody gets a car and gas." He declined. Thus began the well published adventures of New Orleans' founding inspector general. By skillfully and shrewdly building positive relationships with city council members and being readily available to the media, the Inspector General became a public favorite and, with support from city council, the president of Loyola University, Common Good, and other civic leaders, was able to obtain an initial annual operating budget of over \$3M, up from an initially proposed \$250K. He did so by singlehandedly drafting and winning civil service and city council approval of the roster of job descriptions required, in his professional opinion, to staff a credible office. For reasons both of symbolism and security, he established the OIG outside City Hall, in the New Orleans Federal Reserve Bank, and began to hire the approved staff. With fully intended irony and a keen sense of local public interest, the OIG's first investigation was of city vehicles. To no one's surprise, the resulting report found widespread waste and abuse, and made recommendations to bring the city's policies into line with recognized good practices in the administration of a city's motor pool.

Despite professing support periodically for the establishment of the OIG, it would be an understatement to say that Mayor Nagin's administration did not use its authority to facilitate setting up the newly approved office. On the contrary, in one memorable instance, the administration took several months to purchase the computers required to set up the office, after the funds to do so had been fully approved. This incompetence and/or intentional effort to subvert the office delayed the inspector general's attempts to begin the work of hiring a staff and developing an initial work plan. Subsequent investigations by the OIG contributed to felony pleas by the mayor's former top lieutenant and felony convictions for a businessman who conspired with him in a kickback to receive city contracts.

Believing that business as usual in New Orleans city government could and must be interrupted if the city was to be rebuilt for the benefit of all after the hurricane, citizens and public officials successfully instituted an inspector general's office as a nationally recognized best practice for creating enforceable standards of transparency and accountability for those holding public office. From that day forward, the commitment to reform local public institutions has been grounded, both symbolically and pragmatically, in the Office of Inspector General. That office is the principal lever which civic and business leaders and some government officials are now using to reform the public institutions of our city.

G. Changing the city charter to protect the OIG's independence

The city council members and citizen advocates who had collaborated successfully to pass the OIG ordinance and secure funding for its first year of operation were well aware that every year the mayor could recommend and the city council approve reducing or eliminating funding for the office in the annual city budget. The OIG's effectiveness and sustainability depended not just on its capabilities and accomplishments, but also on protecting it from continually shifting partisan political and patronage interests. This would require a funding mechanism not subject to annual approval or adjustment by the mayor or city council.

Toward that end, Common Good worked with reform-oriented city council members to formulate an amendment to the city charter that, if approved by a majority of voters, would set aside .75% of the city's annual operating budget for the operation of the ERB and OIG. The charter change proposal included a provision negotiated by the council members for the establishment of an office of Independent Police Monitor (IPM) as part of the OIG. The inclusion of the police monitor's office made a broader alliance of citizen groups possible. That alliance featured organizations willing to support the police monitor but passionately committed to the OIG, others willing to support the OIG primarily because it would include an independent police monitor, and some equally supportive of both.

This alignment of interests allowed Common Good to convene a multiracial charter-change alliance that also crossed lines of class and geography three months before the vote for the purpose of educating and turning out voters to support the proposed change. In October 2008 77% of voters supported the proposed charter change, with positive margins in all demographic subgroups. This result meant that adequate and predictable annual funding was guaranteed for the OIG and IPM, and that the OIG's hard-won independence would in turn provide autonomy and political cover for the IPM. Only another majority vote of local citizens for a charter change could undo the offices or reduce their funding. Its advocates had provided the OIG with the maximum degree of protection possible in a local democracy, while simultaneously creating the city's first independent agency overseeing the police department.

The process of establishing and protecting the independence of the OIG described above required three years of sustained public work by organized citizen leaders, some of whom were leaders of congregations, working closely with sympathetic elected and appointed officials.

H. Accomplishments of the Office of Inspector General

Over the past five years, the Office of Inspector General of the City of New Orleans has issued numerous audits, reviews, inspections and evaluations of the finances and performance of city government including: city vehicles, city purchasing, accounts payable and fixed asset control, city collection of hotel-motel taxes, sanitation contracts, and private management of major post-Katrina infrastructure rebuilding projects. It has also produced thirteen public letters calling the attention of the mayor, city council, chief administrative officer and police superintendent to administrative practices leaving the city vulnerable to waste and corruption in areas including: awarding of city contracts, procurement of goods and services, expense reimbursement, electronic monitoring of parolees, disadvantaged business enterprises, and proposed contracts for remodeling the city's municipal auditorium. The office conducted investigations of the New Orleans Public Belt Railroad, French Market Corporation, and the city's crime surveillance cameras. It published a detailed report revealing $2.5M being wasted annually by the city's traffic and municipal courts. These and other investigations led to criminal indictments, resignations, and shutting down or major modifications of the operations of these public entities and programs. More recently the OIG has turned its attention to the functioning of the New Orleans Police Department and, among other things, exposed deep failings in the departments classification and follow-upon rape cases.

Although some continue the attempt to delegitimize the OIG by portraying it as an instrument of whites to check black politicians, the broad sense of public opinion across lines of race, class and geography is that the OIG has become the first effective force to interrupt the New Orleans history of waste, fraud and abuse in city government. The OIG has contributed to that perception by creating a level of transparency that for the first time in the city's history allows city administrators, legal authorities and citizens to hold elected and appointed officials accountable for their stewardship of public resources. The OIG has done what few could have imagined, and none had been able to accomplish before the storm: It has created a growing public expectation that waste, fraud and abuse by elected or appointed officials is much more likely to be exposed, with timely and serious consequences for those who risk misusing public office for personal gain.

III. Reflections on the significance of establishing of the Office of Inspector General from the perspective of the social sciences

With apologies to Alfred North Whitehead, the "aeroplane" called practical theology is powered by people of faith becoming disturbed about something transpiring in their social world that shouldn't be or something not transpiring that should be, and flies on wings of social analysis and theological reflection to its landing in organized action in the world as it is. In this section I want to reflect from the perspective of social science on the effort to reform public institutions by establishing an Office of Inspector General which was fueled by civic, business and government leaders disturbed by waste, fraud and abuse in local government.

The failure of public institutions addressed by Common Good and our business and government partners is, of course, not unique to New Orleans. Corruption, waste and the abuse of power by public institutions are world-wide phenomena with destructive consequences for all they touch. Contemporary studies of institutions in the social sciences, the so-called "new institutionalism," are rich with insights for those attempting to create good public institutions and those interested in why that matters. In this section, I explain four interpretations of institutions and institutional change and draw from them a set of leanings about social change in an attempt to illuminate the process and understand the consequences of establishing the Office of Inspector General. The four are like different vantage points on a sculpture, each yielding a perspective and together filling out the viewer's sense of the whole work. Their implications apply to all cities and to larger units of government as well.

A. Social traps: Public institutions, economic opportunity and social trust

Political scientist Bo Rothstein defines a "social trap" as a situation in which there is insufficient trust to allow members of different groups to cooperate, even when it would plainly serve the interests of all groups if they could do so.[4] Such situations are the result of historical struggles among ethnic, religious or socioeconomic groups over freedom, dignity, power and resources. Racial tensions are a classic example of social traps. Rothstein argues that when a social trap is operating in inter-group relations, it is not possible to overcome it by generating additional social trust by directly building or strengthening relationships in civil society. What creates the social trust necessary to break out of social traps is access to economic opportunity for all who are prepared to work and learn. And that opportunity, in turn, is the product of good public institutions.

A "good public institution" is here defined as one that operates lawfully, fairly, efficiently and effectively. On the link between institutions and social trust, Rothstein writes: "The more trust people have in political and administrative institutions, the more they are inclined to feel social trust in their fellow human beings, or the reverse: the more people believe that other people can generally be trusted, the more they trust in social institutions."[5] He adds: "If people cannot trust that public officials will act according to norms such as impartiality, objectivity, incorruptibility, and non-discrimination, they cannot trust 'people in general' either."[6]

The level of social trust required to break through social traps by cooperative inter-group relations is created indirectly via good public institutions that make economic opportunity available fairly. How people in general view the integrity of the public officials administering and enforcing institutional rules shapes how they view the general trustworthiness of their fellow citizens: "If it proves that I cannot trust the local police, judges, teachers, and doctors, then whom in this society can I trust?"[7]

The case study above details the creation of a city office constitutionally mandated and funded to promote good public institutions. In the light of the concept of social traps and their solution, the Office of Inspector General can be seen as a powerful instrument for taking two critical steps that must be taken for the well being of New Orleans as a whole, and, indeed, the common good of any city. First, community leaders committed to increasing economic opportunity for all who are willing to learn and work must see to it that local public institutions serve all entitled to their protection and services lawfully, fairly, efficiently and effectively. As noted in the previous section, these are the behaviors of local government that make businesses and citizens believe that investing in a city's future makes sense. It is also the case that those who face the biggest economic challenges are also the ones who most need government services, because it is difficult if not impossible for them to provide privately for education, health care, neighborhood security, etc. Absent good public institutions as defined here, the politics and economics of any city will continue to be degraded into power struggles among actual and would-be insiders, while access to opportunity for outsiders continues to diminish.

Second, New Orleans leaders committed to create the institutional conditions that promote expanding economic opportunity for all by establishing the OIG have also put themselves on the most powerful path to build social trust among groups that have been divided by conflict. No form or amount of multiracial, interfaith and cross-class dialogue and education about racism, intolerance or class conflict, or multiracial social events will add significantly to the city's reservoir of inter-group trust as long as people continue to be favored or limited in achieving economic success because they belong or don't belong to particular groups.

In summary, good public institutions are a direct link to increasing economic opportunity for all and an indirect link to building social trust among historically divided groups. Public institutions, economic opportunity, and social trust go together, for better and for worse. The OIG is a powerful influence now available to strengthen both links in New Orleans.

B. The triadic structure of institutions: Rules, norms, enforcement

In the previous section, I outlined one view of the critical role that public institutions play in the creation or destruction of economic opportunity for all and social trust among groups. But what is an "institution," exactly? In the technical sense employed here, the word "institution" denotes "a set of rules." It is not interchangeable, as in everyday language, with the word "organization." Nobel laureate economist Douglass North outlines a triadic model of institutions as an interlocking set of rules, norms and enforcement mechanisms.[8]

In the life of the city of New Orleans, *rules* encompass a constitution (city charter), laws (ordinances) and policies, including a code of ethics. City rules are nested within state and national rules (constitutions and laws) and subject to their constraints. As we have seen in the case above, the New Orleans city charter had mandated an inspector general's office for a decade before Katrina, but no such entity independent of the mayor's office had been established. This rule was waiting to be implemented by ordinance of the city council, with no changes to the city charter or new state legislation required. Following its establishment by ordinance and initial funding, proponents of the OIG successfully led an effort to amend the city charter to protect the OIG's existence and funding from decisions of future mayors and city councils. Their success meant that the office could be undone only by another majority vote of citizens to change the city charter. Working within the existing rules to establish the office and later moving to change the rules to protect it were part of the intentional strategy of civic, business and government leaders supporting reform of city government in New Orleans after the hurricane.

North defines *norms* as personally internalized rules. The rules of the Code of Ethics of the City of New Orleans and the State of Louisiana forbid self-dealing, i.e., using public office for personal gain, by elected and appointed officials. Nonetheless, self-dealing by New Orleans public officials has been widespread historically, and accepted by many as "just the way things are here." Prior to Hurricane Katrina, official rules against self-dealing had not become effectively motivating norms for many public officials, or for the citizenry as a whole. The establishment of the OIG has begun to move the city and state codes of ethics from rules on paper to guidelines in the working consciences of public officials and citizens. Appropriate and effective norms come from good rules, effective enforcement, visible leadership by key public officials committed to following those rules, and ethics education for public officials, city employees, contractors and citizens. Such education works best not by asking people to memorize and regurgitate ethics rules, but rather by allowing them to grasp those rules by exploring specific, expectable conflicts for those in various positions from mayor's office to street crews. The city's Ethics Review Board is now leading the effort to create an ethics education process based on national best practices for the public officials, city workers, contractors doing business with the city, and citizens.

According to North's model, effective rules and norms depend on successful *enforcement*. The function of an OIG is prevention and detection of waste, fraud and abuse by public officials, city workers, contractors and citizens. Starkly put, the prevention of such behaviors depends upon creating a constant and credible threat of exposure and sanctions for those disbursing and receiving public resources. The role of enforcement is to create that threat. Since its establishment, the New Orleans OIG has become a powerful source of negative consequences for those who would abuse public office and public resources. To date those consequences range from federal indictments and convictions of a former high-ranking city official and a vendor for a kickback scheme involving the city's crime cameras, to exposing fiduciary failure by executive directors and members of boards and commissions overseeing public funds, leading to resignations, re-imbursement and restructuring. The days when self-dealing was routinely expected of public officials and contractors have been abruptly interrupted by the OIG's effective use of the credible threat of exposure and sanctions as a means of enforcement against those who choose to violate the public trust.

One encouraging sign of the effectiveness of the OIG to date can be found in an explicit written directive from the city's chief administrative officer ordering all city workers to comply promptly with all OIG requests for information. This unambiguous administration requirement of all city employees is a new rule, one that is likely to influence the norms of those working for the city because all signs indicate that it will be enforced.

In Koch's account of the institution called "the gate," we can identify North's three constitutive elements of an institution: *rules* (e.g., "the Israelite constitution," including the provision that only "free, adult men" had legal standing at the gate), *norms* (e.g., fairness in allotting taxes, compulsory labor and military service) and *enforcement* (e.g., pronouncing judgment in family matters and capital cases). At these ancient gates, communities managed disputes, administered justice, cared for their places of worship, set taxes, and divided communal responsibilities. What we would today call "local government" happened at the gate. The Amos text also describes a pattern familiar to the modern reader—ancient insider dealing by larger and wealthier families who stacked the local council and used their voting majority to establish taxes in a manner that favored their interests to the detriment of less numerous and wealthy families, in plain violation of the command to establish justice in the gate.

C. The role of ideas in institutional change

When institutions are disrupted by political strife, citizen organizing or natural disasters, the ideas people have at their disposal are critical for their analysis of what is transpiring, possible outcomes and their respective desirability, and possible bases for consensus among different (and often differing) interested parties. "Ideas" encompass both theoretical concepts like Keynesian vs. Neo-conservative economics and the working understandings of public officials and ordinary citizens.

Social theorist Mark Blyth describes a specific temporal sequence in the role that ideas play in times of institutional change. He proposes that ideas 1.) allow actors in times of institutional disequilibrium to interpret the nature of the crisis they face; 2.) function as resources for collective action and building coalitions; 3.) serve as weapons for attacking and delegitimizing existing institutions; 4.) become blueprints for new institutions; and 5.) allow the newly institutionalized ideas to stabilize the new institutions. He notes that: "In understanding the role of ideas in institutional change, sequence is everything."[9]

Tracing Blyth's sequence in the establishment of the New Orleans OIG reveals two sets of ideas in conflict throughout the process and that continue to generate social tension: "reform" vs. "white take-over."

The initial role of ideas in times of crisis is to give actors a way of interpreting the situation in which they must act. In the aftermath of Katrina's abrupt rupture of business and politics as usual in New Orleans, one group of leaders saw the opportunity to recreate the city for the benefit of all by reforms promoting lawful, fair, efficient and effective public institutions, while another saw "so-called reform" as an opportunistic power grab by the "white shadow government," an attack on black political power by the white minority. The conflicting ideas of "reform" vs. "white take-over" were the frames within which their respective adherents would interpret the effort to establish the OIG, and support or oppose it accordingly.

Having allowed actors to interpret the nature of the crisis they face, ideas then serve as resources for collective action and building coalitions. In the unsettled post-Katrina environment, a diverse alliance of civic, government and business leaders rallied to the idea of a New Orleans free of patronage and corruption and pressed effectively for establishment of an OIG. Those who opposed "so-called reform" on racial grounds would argue that they were unable to organize an effective counter-alliance because many of their constituents had not returned to New Orleans. A more important reason for their failure, however, was that the perception of patronage and corruption as endemic and profoundly damaging to the future prospects of the city of New Orleans was shared broadly enough across lines of race, religion and class, that it could not be effectively countered by playing the race card.

Having given actors a basis for collective action in the situation, ideas also serve as weapons for attacking and delegitimizing existing institutions. In challenging waste and corruption in city government by supporting the OIG, the reform alliance took the principled position that patronage and cronyism by white public officials when whites held political power in New Orleans was wrong and did not justify black officials continuing those practices. Those in opposition had only one argument for reinstating the pre-Katrina status quo: In a majority black city, many of those who had been previously marginalized by a white majority felt that were entitled to continue controlling public institutions and deploying their resources as they saw fit, so long as public officials were democratically elected and appointed per the terms of the city's charter and ordinances. More crudely put: "We're the majority and we have the right to control the public trough now, just like you did. As usual, you're trying to change the rules when it's our turn."

Having served as a basis for undoing old institutions, ideas then become blueprints for new ones. The Kennedy School's identification of an inspector general's office as the national best practice for cities attempting to address waste and corruption gave OIG advocates access to a model for the functioning of an inspector general in the form of the "Green Book" of rules and procedures adopted by the national Association of Inspectors General, as well as an office organized per those principles as a model, the Office of the Inspector General of Miami/Dade County. Opponents responded with an effort to discredit those organizations by including them in the attack on the "white shadow government's" attempt to take back control of city government.

Newly institutionalized ideas help stabilize the new institutions they have helped to create by affecting what people now expect of their institutions. The body of work produced by the OIG to date feeds a growing public perception of the office's independence from local politics. Indeed, the OIG is the only local public institution for which such a claim can be made credibly. That perception is fueling the hope and expectation that the old days of clear sailing for those using public office in New Orleans with impunity to benefit themselves and their cronies are finished. Opponents continue to the attempt to discredit the OIG as an instrument of white power, but the same argument which proved insufficient to stop the establishment of the OIG and its enshrinement in the city charter, appears to be losing whatever persuasive force it may have had among all but the most ideological of racial opponents.

The case of the establishment of the Office of Inspector General supports Blyth's assertion that in times of profound institutional disruption, ideas have specific consequences as change is attempted and contested. For the first six months of this effort, the response of even progressive business and civic leaders to the idea of an inspector general in New Orleans ranged from an amused shake of the head to "In New Orleans? You must be crazy!" One local media figure opined that a functioning inspector general would be the "biggest change in New Orleans since the Civil War." Six years after the Government Efficiency and Effectiveness Committee of the Bring New Orleans Back Commission first put the inspector general on the horizon of possibility of the local citizenry, the cynics have new ideas representing new possibilities to consider and the media representative's words may yet prove to be prescient.

D. Creating and sustaining the public good of good public institutions

Put positively, the purpose of an inspector general is to enhance lawfulness, fairness, efficiency and effectiveness in city government. Clearly these are good institutional qualities, but precisely what kind of good are they? Social scientist Elinor Ostrom offers a model of four kinds of goods based on their accessibility and subtractability.[10] *Private goods* are diminished when appropriated and all others are excluded from using them (e.g., a privately owned home or a tank of gas purchased for one's personal vehicle). *Toll goods* are not diminished by use but some people can be excluded from using them (e.g., toll roads and concert tickets). *Common-pool resources* are diminished by use but most people are excluded from using them (e.g., a village's forest or the water supply of a group of farmers). *Public goods* are not diminished by use and no one is excluded from using them (e.g., safe streets, clean air).

Public goods such as safe streets are *like* common-pool resources such as a communal forest, in that both can be managed so that all with legitimate access get what they need on a sustainable basis. Public goods such as safe streets are *not like* common-pool resources in that all have legitimate access to them. Given this similarity and difference between two kinds of goods, it is instructive to consider how what has been learned about managing common-pool resources around the world might assist those attempting to create the public good which is the focus of this essay, that is, good—lawful, fair, efficient and effective—public institutions.

Research summarized by Ostrom and her colleagues highlights the effects of a number of variables on the success or failure of groups organizing voluntarily to manage common-pool resources. One finding of that research is that such efforts are more likely to be successful when stakeholders have the local autonomy to create and enforce their own rules. Lacking that autonomy, local stakeholders attempting to organize voluntarily may find themselves blocked by opponents' appeals to officials with significant legal authority, like mayors or governors. By contrast, "with the legal autonomy to make their own rules, users face substantially lower costs in defending their own rules against other authorities."[11]

Those seeking initially to create the public good of good local institutions by establishing the Office of Inspector General in New Orleans had only to point out to reform-minded post-Katrina city council candidates that the local rules already in place in the city charter included the requirement that an OIG be established. That charter provision gave city council members, spurred on by engaged citizens, the autonomy and responsibility to enact the required city legislation. No changes in state laws or constitution were necessary. By contrast, another important post-Katrina reform of local public institutions, the consolidation of seven local tax assessors into one, required a state-wide majority vote to change the Louisiana constitution. The latter reform was a successful, but also a much more costly undertaking involving, among other expenses, state-wide television and radio ads. As described above, the local autonomy of the Office of Inspector General was decisively strengthened two years after its establishment when its initial proponents and their allies successfully led a campaign resulting in a city-wide majority vote to amend the city charter to provide substantial funding for the OIG on an annual basis without approval of the mayor or city council. Only another city-wide majority vote could close or de-fund the OIG by changing the city charter. The public good of good public institutions created by the inspector general's office is the result of local organizing affecting the city charter and ordinances, rather than the exercise of state or federal legal authority.

E. Good institutions, good ideas, and public goods: Implications for doing practical theology

What are the implications of the foregoing social scientific perspectives for those engaged in social analysis as part of doing practical theology?

Rothstein's analysis of the effects of public institutions highlights the larger social significance of lawful, fair, efficient and effective institutions for the well being of cities by making plain the links among the quality of a city's public institutions, the generation or limitation of economic opportunity for all, and social trust among groups. Public institutions, economic opportunity for all, and inter-group trust spiral up or down together.

North's account of the triadic structure of institutions teaches would-be reformers that rules, norms and enforcement must function together if citizens and public officials intend to establish and maintain good public institutions. For example, without effective enforcement rules are irrelevant and norms ineffectual. His analysis reinforces the guiding strategic idea that social action partnerships of civic, business and government leaders could bring transparency and accountability by establishing, funding and protecting an office with the capacity to enforce rules and create norms of lawfulness, fairness, efficiency and effectiveness in local public institutions.

Blyth's analysis shows a sequence of roles that ideas can play in institutional change. Whether their locales have faced a natural disaster or not, local leaders in civic, business, and government sectors face the challenge of attacking serious and longstanding problems like violent crime, failing public schools, and government corruption and waste. Having guided collective action in the immediate post-Katrina situation, the ideas about public institutions explained above have become blueprints for the future of public institutions, not only in New Orleans, but other places as well. They do so by helping to create, first among reform leaders and then the larger public, the expectation that nothing less than lawfulness, fairness, efficiency and effectiveness are acceptable in local public institutions.

Finally, Ostrom's analysis of how people have managed common-pool goods while maintaining their viability teaches those seeking to create fully public goods like a lawful, fair, efficient and effective city hall or criminal justice system to pay shrewd attention to the ways in which city, state and federal rules can be both levers for and barriers to local institutional reform by enhancing or impeding local autonomy.

Citizen-led action to change public institutions is a complex but not incomprehensible process. Those committed to economic opportunity for all and peace among social groups, including those who would do practical theology, must develop a practical understanding of how collective action.

IV. What has the effort to "establish justice in the gate" by creating an office of inspector general taught us about creating the critical public good of good public institutions?

The first five learnings in this section are drawn from the author's reflections on the sustained collective effort described in the case study above of the effort to establish and protect the Office of Inspector General as the critical lever for reforming the institutions of local government in New Orleans following Hurricane Katrina. In my experience, they speak to all efforts to organize for social change, including those that fall under the rubric of practical theology.

1.) Change aimed at the benefit of all in a city requires recruiting and sustaining as diverse a group of partners as possible, but without giving up the capacity to act effectively together. This inevitably means not inviting some potential participants. In a democracy, everyone has a right to participate in social action partnerships, but not everyone can do so constructively.

2.) Focusing on a limited number of wisely chosen "whats," and exercising the shared discipline to hold that limited focus and adjust tactics until success is achieved and/or capacity grows, is a hallmark of effective social action partnerships. Organizing efforts that try to do it all, or do too much, will accomplish little and unravel.

3.) Mutual accountability is a requirement of effective social action partnerships. It requires that every task taken on by such partnerships is someone's responsibility within a specified time frame and has an appropriate outcome indicator and that partners hold each other accountable for commitments made.

4.) Organizations, coalitions, alliances and movements are different ways of coming together to accomplish valued social outcomes. The challenge is to choose the form that fits current purposes and circumstances. This is a pragmatic decision requiring neither theoretical nor technical but rather practical wisdom. A network approach to social action partnerships allows for informal, flexible coordination of all three.

5.) A powerful organizing strategy for changing a city for the good of all is organizing focused, sustained tri-sector action partnerships of government, business and civic leaders within in a flexible and open social action network, one that can respond rapidly to constantly changing challenges and opportunities.

The next four learnings are drawn from the theoretical analyses of institutions by social scientists presented above.

6.) Those committed to economic opportunity for all, as well as to respectful public relationships among members of different groups, can do nothing more powerful than requiring good— that is lawful, fair, efficient and effective—public institutions.

7.) Good public institutions entail specific rules and internalized norms, the effectiveness of which, in turn, depends on credible enforcement.

8.) The ideas that citizens and public officials have about how public institutions, economic opportunity and social trust go together, making possible and limiting their capacity to produce the public goods of economic opportunity and social peace.

9.) The public good of good public institutions can be created and sustained by those who have or acquire the autonomy to create and enforce the necessary rules.

As I noted above, practical theology is powered by people of faith becoming disturbed about something transpiring in their social world that shouldn't be or something not transpiring that should be, and flies on wings of social analysis and theological reflection to its landing in organized action in the world as it is. Social change for the common good must be adequately fueled or motivated and shrewdly aimed. Prophetic texts like Amos' mandate to establish justice in the gate can power efforts like the one described here to make their cities and societies just and merciful. Such classic prophetic texts motivate actors by continually reminding them of the ultimate meaning of organizing for change, that is, that God and humans share joint covenantal responsibility for establishing justice in history. Social analysis guides efforts at social change in practical ways, helping people of faith and citizens to organize and aim their actions wisely. Religious and ethical traditions supply the "why" for doing practical theology, organizing principles and social analysis the "how," and people's consciences the "what."

1 Klaus Koch. *The Prophets (I): The Assyrian Period.* Philadelphia, Fortress Press, 1983.

2 Edward Chambers & Michael Cowan. *Roots for Radicals.* New York: Continuum, 2005. Klaus Koch. *The Prophets (I): The Assyrian Period.* Philadelphia, Fortress Press, 1983.

3 Huston Smith. *The World's Religions.* New York: Harpers and Row, 1985.

4 Bo Rothstein. *Social Traps and the Problem of Trust.* Cambridge: Cambridge University Press, 2005.

5 Rothstein, p. 111.

6 Rothstein, p. 120.

7 Rothstein, p. 122.

8 Douglass North. *Institutions, Institutional Change and Economic Performance.* Cambridge: Cambridge University Press, 1990.

9 Mark Blythe. *Great Transformations: Economic Ideas and Political Change in the Twentieth Century.* Cambridge: Cambridge University Press, 2006.

10 Amy Poteete, Marco Janssen, and Elinor Ostrom. *Working Together: Collective Action, the Commons, and Multiple Methods in Practice.* Princeton: Princeton University Press, 2010.

11 Poteete, Janssen & Ostrom, p. 241.

Chapter 10

Narratives, Margins and Meanings

On Learning with Bernard Lee

William V. D'Antonio

I begin this reflection on my socio-theological learning experience with Bernard Lee with several readings, not to be confused with the daily lectionary. The first is from his *The Catholic Experience of Small Christian Communities,* Chapter 5, Perspectives and Portents: Theological Interpretations and Pastoral Recommendations.

> At the beginning of this chapter, I offer the metaphor of *margins* to locate small Christian communities in the contemporary Catholic Church. On a page from a book, the margins are the open space on all sides of the text. But if anyone scribbles thoughts in the margins, it's hard to read the printed text as if there were no comments. I will suggest that SCCs are like jottings in the margins of a text, where text means *the church.* . . . .(Lee, 2000, 117)[1] . . . "Things written or drawn in the margins add an extra dimension, a supplement, that is able to gloss, parody, modernize and problematize the text's authority while never totally undermining it."[2] (Camille,1992).

The second reading is also from Bernard Lee, in *Habits for the Journey*.

> Based on our research, it is our judgment that the current small community movement in this country needs to learn that any true ecclesial community is both gathered and sent. In our recent book on Small Christian Communities, Michael Cowan and I observed for gospel reasons and for sociological reasons that SCCs in this country will be a blip on the screen of ecclesial history rather than an engaging, strong narrative, if communities do not have proactive conversation with the world beyond their community membership, as well as effective mutual conversation with each other.

Gathered and sent. The gathering does the sending. The sending calls for gathering.[3] My third reading is taken from a paper by Gerard Moore, S.M., "A Spirituality for Justice."

> How do we foster the spirit of justice within us? How do we nurture it? There are many ways we act justly. There are many ways we leave untouched considerations of justice. Often enough, we turn a blind eye to insights and thoughts that have come to us, that have found their way into our minds. Underneath these dynamics is another question. How do I become a person who is attentive to the spirit of justice and moved by that same spirit to act? Among the answers to the question are to be found the touchstones of a spirituality of justice. Acting justly, and acting for justice on behalf of others, is a spiritual quest. It is a response to the promptings of the Holy Spirit at work in our hearts.[4]

A word about Gerard Moore. He was for many years a Marist priest theologian, now married, who lives in Australia. He spent several years at the Washington Theological Union, while living at the Marist College. Through Sister Maureen Healy, the pastoral administrator of the Intentional Eucharistic Community (IEC) to which my wife and I belonged, Communitas, Gerard frequently was the priest presider at our Sunday Mass. Over time we became friends. He was a strong supporter of the Small Christian Community (SCC) movement in general, and especially of the more marginal IEC part of the general movement.

My fourth reading is from the writings of Robert K. Merton, one of the 20th century's leading intellectuals, a truly gifted sociologist. For many sociologists he is a gospel writer of sorts:

> The narratives [that constitute the stories of our lives] and their interpretations tell of reference groups and reference individuals, the significant others that helped shape the changing character of thought and inquiry. . . . Full-fledged sociological autobiographers relate their intellectual development both to changing social and cognitive micro-environments provided by the larger society and culture....Such accounts bear witness that one's experiences and foci of interest, one's accomplishments and failures, were in no small part a function of the historical moment at which one has entered the field.[5]

Now to the readings. Bernard writes about margins, and quotes other scholars who think of book margins in a variety of important ways. I had never thought about book margins other than as places to write in and on, that is, before learning about them from Bernard. I happen to be a margin writer; I find myself often in dialogue or disagreement with the author, and I use the margins to say so. Occasionally, I have done so with books borrowed from the library. But I had never thought of or read anything about margins as a metaphor for anything, much less the SCC movement. Then I discovered in one of the early exchanges between Bernard, Michael and the rest of us that Michael had listed our Communitas as in the margins. And now a word about IECs as in the margins.

Beginning in 1991, a year before I met Bernard and Mike Cowan in person, Maureen Healy organized the first gathering of IECs, as we think of ourselves. Maureen knew Bernard and Mike, and arranged to have them address our Gathering via a VCR tape. That is how I came to meet Bernard and Mike, on the film. Members from 18 IECs from all parts of the country attended this gathering, held at the Washington Theological Union in May of 1991. We have since held two more gatherings, in May 2001, and again in May of 2009. Close to 300 people from 45 IECS were in attendance in 2009; I am sure some if not most would think of themselves as in the margins. More see themselves as prophetic, especially as a growing number now are led by ordained women priests. We do not determine which groups are IECs. If the community has the celebration of the Eucharist as its central form of worship, and wishes to be listed, it is listed. Our IEC web site now has a list of about 150 communities that identify themselves as IECs. Based on my own casual contacts and research activity since 2000, I would not be surprised if there were at least 1,000 such communities, reflecting a range of liturgical formats, some being very much within the institutional framework of the Church, others less so, and some very much in the margins. But my main purpose is not to probe exactly what the margins might mean in the case of these IECs. One of the most interesting things from my knowledge about them based on a national survey of IECs is that they, more than any other SCCs I know about, are conscious of and dedicate a great amount of time, energy, and money to being sent. I will cite one example later in my reflection.

So my question is not about the survival of SCCs of one type or another, but rather one about their ability to be sent. After reflecting on all the data and especially the observations and interviews that we carried out, I would say the following: Small communities gradually become comfortable with each other over a period from 3 to 5 years, depending on whether they meet weekly, bi-weekly or monthly. The more frequently they meet, the sooner they bond, and within three years, they typically care enough about each other to be concerned about how to help out in health and other emergencies.

SCCs move beyond this first stage, which I think of as becoming a neo-family support group to a second stage, which includes visiting the sick in hospitals, visiting people in prison, weekly soup kitchen activity, and such other demonstrations of concern for the local community, but not an attempt to change structures.

Gathering and being sent: An example of an SCC in North Carolina

The Friday Night Community of Charlotte was the most complete community that I interviewed. Not only did they gather and do so with a level of total commitment that was most unusual, but they were also sent or sent themselves at levels both interfamilial and structural within the larger community in a way that meets the criteria of social justice as Gerard Moore framed them.

The Friday Night Gathering opened with a meal, after all were there and we were introduced and I spoke briefly about our project. Someone led an opening prayer as the candle was lit; that was followed by a reading from the Sunday scriptures. This was followed by commentary which led into some faith sharing, and then the leader brought that part of the gathering to an end. The focus moved to the local bishop and the public reaction to the play "Angels over America," playing in the Charlotte area at that time. It became clear that they were pleased with the bishop's positive reaction to the play and with his public support of it against some local criticism. Someone moved that the community's secretary prepare a letter thanking the bishop for his support of the play and the theater, and all directly involved. There was a unanimous vote in favor of the motion. There was then a second motion that each individual member of the community write the bishop to thank him for his stand on the play. Again, there was unanimous approval.

The next item was the end of school busing in Charlotte. A conservative group was mounting a campaign to end busing of children that had been a model for helping to insure integration of the public schools in the region. The pitch was that busing had served its purpose and was no longer needed, and that taxpayers would save millions of dollars a year. Apparently several members of this Friday Night Community had been active in trying to find out as much as they could, especially about whom else in Charlotte shared their concerns. Someone mentioned several actions that had been taken to forestall this move. It seemed probable that the anti-busers would prevail. Several fallback positions were discussed: apparently there was or would be an opening on the City Council. So there followed discussion of their chances of finding a candidate whom they and other like groups could support.

Someone who had already had contacts with other progressive groups supporting busing volunteered to expand the contacts, ascertain their desire to work together, and move to the next step. That led someone to report on several church groups that were organizing within the city to insure that in the new drawing of the school lines, the effort to insure continued integration would prevail. There was discussion of what other groups were likely to work with them.

After spelling out their strategy on the busing issue, they turned to internal matters again. The daughter of one of the members was in serious condition from cancer. They discussed ways to help the family. They promised prayers, and here I was surprised to hear someone ask if the prayer group of the local Charismatic community had been contacted for their special prayers. I had just interviewed one of the leaders of the local Charismatic Community a couple of nights earlier, and had learned about their special prayer groups. Someone agreed to contact the Charismatic community. Finally, there was a concluding prayer, and the candle was put out.

In the discussion that followed, I learned that three of the community's members held Ph.D.s and several had experience with local government. All seemed to have college degrees and some to have had much of their education in Catholic schools. This SCC was listed as associated with Call to Action. It did not meet as a community for Sunday liturgy, and was not attached to a single parish. Its members came from all over the city.

Two years later in preparation for this essay, and out of sheer curiosity, I decided to see what I could learn about what happened to the Charlotte-Mecklenburg School District's Busing program. So I typed in to the computer "Charlotte District School Busing." My computer produced a nineteen page document. A quotation from the page one tells all: "Something is different about the children gazing out the windows of the yellow school buses lumbering up Selwyn Elementary School's driveway. Most of the black faces are gone." (Source: Adversity.Net/ education_2_north_carolina.htm.) The report stated that in 1999 the parents of a then six year old daughter had filed a law suit against the school district because she had been denied a seat in a gifted program because all the slots set aside for non-Black children had been filled. There was no indication in the 19 pages that the suit against the busing program was designed to save several million dollars a year.

My interview and visit with the Friday night community took place in 1997. The judge's decision to end the busing program was handed down on September 10, 1999. A three judge appeals panel reversed the decision a year later, and then the U.S. Court of Appeals overruled the three judge panel. Busing for integration of the races finally ended in in 2002, and the new student-to-school assignment began in 2004. This case was of particular interest because from the 1970s to the 1990s Charlotte-Mecklenburg was hailed as an example of a school district that made desegregation work. It is at moments like that that I wish I were 15 years younger with a research grant to find out what had happened to the SCC members with whom I had spent an evening 15 years ago.

To conclude this part of my chapter: It appeared to me that the Friday Night Community was focused on an issue of social justice, as they understood it, and tried to take a stand. No one talked directly about spirituality that night in 1997, but in retrospect, their behavior seemed to me to be spirit-filled. This brings me back to Gerard Moore's statement about spirituality, and about gathering and being sent.

As we were preparing the last part of our study of SCCs, which would involve both participant observation and interviews with SCC members, such as the one discussed above, Bernard and his theologian colleagues said it would be important to ask questions about what the term spirituality meant to members as individuals, and how their membership in SCCs affected their spiritual life.

My first reaction was that trying to get empirical data from interviews on concepts like spirituality and spiritual life seemed impossible to me. Those terms were not part of my vocabulary. I realized I really was uncomfortable with the term. But at this point, I also realized that the concept was important to Bernard and his colleagues, and after all, Bernard had raised the money, and was paying my expenses to visit and talk to all these interesting people. So we included the terms in the interview schedule.

On April 30, 1997, I met with five members of the Immaculate Heart Community of Los Angeles. They also had listed themselves as associated with Call to Action, and that is where we found their name and brief description. I have maintained contact with the Immaculate Heart

Community, and now think of them as an IEC rather than an SCC. They are definitely in the margins.

The leader of the group I met with was Dr. Anita Caspary, known as the "Rebel nun" who led the community in its struggle with Cardinal McIntyre and his demands: 1) that all the women religious would have to return to wearing the most traditional habits, 2) they would have to revise their approaches to classroom teaching and course content, and remove the signs of worldliness that had infected their order. As one of the sisters stated: "their questions to us were insulting, as they tried to penetrate into our personal, spiritual lives." Their struggle with the Cardinal was primarily over the meaning of the word "obedience," as it is now, again, for so many Catholics, women religious or not. For Cardinal McIntyre, obedience simply meant that Catholics were expected to accept whatever he demanded as the rule to be followed literally. It meant accepting his demand that the women return to their old Habits (Big H and little h). As they explained to me, they looked into the abyss and determined after much discernment that "obedience has to do with hearing the word of God." They informed me that the core root of the word obedience has to do with hearing and not necessarily obeying what some other human being or group of people are telling you to do. As Sister Anita said, looking into the abyss, they found the courage to follow their conscience and continue to dissent from the Cardinal's demands, which were later reinforced by demands from Rome. In 1970, they formed the Immaculate Heart Community as an independent community, their lawyers worked out a cash settlement with the ten percent of sisters who wished to remain with the church charter. The settlement was approved by the Cardinal. Of the 500 plus members in the Order in 1966, when the struggle began, there were 350 who joined the new community.

With those remarks as background, I now turn to what happened when I finally asked the five women a version of the question, "What does the word "spirituality" mean to you?" I asked these five members of the Immaculate Heart Community how the struggle with the Cardinal and the Vatican had changed their lives. (The details of their struggle with Cardinal McIntyre and the bishops and priests who represented him in negotiations with the IHC are available in their archives and elsewhere.)

So I asked: "How has being a part of this community changed your spiritual life? Does it affect your religious life at all? Has it deepened your spiritual life?"

One member replied: "One of the ways I like to think about my own spiritual life is in relationship with the world around me. And what this community does for me is call forth who I am as a Christian, as a Catholic. It helps me to recognize who God is in my world, and how I participate in this world as who I am, as who I am called to be in this world. And I do that in relationship with you as we come to talk about who we are as a community, with my sisters or my brothers. So, for me, spirituality is a part of being a member of the community. Certainly, I owe a lot to this community because of the education I have been afforded and the importance that the community placed on education of its members theologically, philosophically, spiritually."

I then asked: "What does it mean to have a spiritual life? What does it mean to a woman religious to have a spiritual life?"

Another member replied: "My feeling is that our spirituality is not that different because we are Immaculate Heart Community. Spiritual life used to be really self-contained and really small within the convent wall. Go to your room and read a passage from a book, and try to achieve a transcendent relationship with God. Highly individual."

I then asked, "What are you doing when you are being spiritual? Are you praying as a group?

A third speaker said: "You are seeing and searching for the reality of God in everything, persons, nature, the cosmos." The second speaker added: "I didn't mean to limit spirituality to the community because, for me, the community has opened up. And a part of opening up a spirituality to the cosmos, you know, if we can get that broad, is our participation as a community in the world around us through the kinds of Justice and Peace activities that go on."

And I asked, "Those are acts that reflect your spirituality?"

The second speaker replied: "I hope so."

The third added: "Sure. Sure. I think your spirituality is to live out the gospel. And you know, when Jesus said, "Feed the Hungry". . . Whatever we do in our lives, whether it's in relationships, how I think I'm living it out while I am teaching a class, I mean we're doing the environment now. My mother used to say 'Everything I do is a prayer.' So every living moment is living out our call to be faithful to the gospel and I think that spirituality is not compartmentalized, it's the fabric of our lives."

The first speaker commented: "I think as a community we very early had an idea that everything we do is holy, and that was exemplified by certain leadership in the community. On the other hand, there was the kind of withdrawal and a 'I'm a nun and I'm holy in a special way, and I have to pray certain hours.' And then with Vatican II, the open kind of spirituality, the daily kind of spirituality, which doesn't mean so many hours of prayer, but that everything is a prayer, kind of took over."

The first speaker then gave an account of two young women who had come to apply for a teaching position that was open, and they both came to Mass. "It happens that one of the nuns who leads the prayers of intentions at Offertory time always begins in a very loud voice with 'For equality for women in the Church,' and I'll respond in a loud voice, 'Lord, hear our prayer.' And then the intentions are for all the souls in purgatory, and then for the Blacks, the Catholics, the pope, and all the other people who need our prayers. And after Mass, this young would-be teacher said to me, 'You certainly have different types of spirituality here.'"

On obedience, the fifth speaker said: I'd just like to comment on obedience because I preach about that all the time. What I preach is that it has to do with hearing the word of God. That's what it is. The core root of that word has to do with hearing and not necessarily obeying what some other person or group are telling you."

I have gone on at length recounting what the women of the Immaculate Heart Community told me in response to my questions about spirituality in their lives. I did so because this interview had such an impact on me. For the first time I felt I was beginning to understand the meaning of being spiritual, or one way of being spiritual, and that this was a spirituality I was trying to live, without recognizing it. Slowly it dawned on me why I was moved by the ancient Latin chant, "*Ubi caritas et amor, Deus ibi est.*" I suppose it is no accident that Sister Maureen Healy, who had introduced me to Bernard, had also introduced the chant as one of our Communion hymns at Communitas.

As a result of this revelation, if you will, I began to look for ways to talk about or ask people about what being spiritual meant to them. A major opportunity occurred with our Third Gathering of Intentional Eucharistic Communities (IECs) in 2009. Fr. Ted Keating, A Marist priest, and strong supporter of IECs in the Washington, D.C. area, suggested that we have a major session devoted to how IEC members perceived the idea of being religious and/or being spiritual. So we constructed a series of questions and created a representative sample of members from the IECs on the list we had been building over the years. It yielded a rich array of comments, and some in-depth statements from a number of respondents.

We also included a series of questions on the religious-spiritual dialogue in our 2011 survey of American Catholics, from which I have created the tables below. A more detailed examination of the findings also appears in the chapters of *American Catholics in Transition.*[6]

In our 2011 survey we asked if the respondents had been members of RENEW, SCCs, IECs, and/or Hispanic small groups. The percentage of the respondents who said they were or are members of those small faith communities were RENEW 7 %, SCCs 15%, IECs 4%, Hispanic/Latino 9%. For this chapter, I focus on our findings about those who had been or still are members of SCCs. We removed the Hispanic members from the list so that the SCC members on whom I am reporting in the tables below are White, non-Hispanic SCC members. In the tables I compare the White SCC members with the rest of the white population in our survey. I also make an occasional comparison with the white SCC members reported on in *The Catholic Experience of Small Christian Communities.* We did not have any questions that would directly reflect on whether and to what extent the SCC members are Sent as well as Gathered. Table 1.1 provides a demographic profile of SCCs and the general white population.

Table 1.1: Percentages of SCC members compared with rest of white population

By generation	SCCs	Population
Pre-Vatican II	25%	12%
Vatican II	31	35
Post-Vatican II	28	34
Millennial	16	19
Gender	SCCs	Population
Female	53	51

Male	47	49
Current marriage approved by the Church	84	67
Spouse is Catholic	89	71
Catholic School Education		
Elementary	53	45
High School	31	29
College	28	8
Political Party Affiliation		
Republican	19	30
Democratic	31	33
Independent	50	38
Mass Attendance		
At least weekly	66	24

Table 1.1: Percentages of SCC members compared with rest of white population (cont.)

At least monthly	21	19
Seldom/Never	13	57
Level of Commitment to the Catholic Church		
Low	3	17
Medium	52	67
High	42	16

More than half of the SCCs are drawn from the two oldest generations while in the population at large the two younger generations are a majority. Our findings reported on in 2000 showed a similar distribution with a slight majority (52%) in the two older generations. Gender differences are not significant in the current study, while in 2000 the ratio was 8 women to 5 men. Regarding Catholic education it is at the Catholic college level that SCC members have led the way, 28 percent to 8 percent.

SCC members are more Democratic than the population as a whole, and that holds also at the national level based on all recent polls. The most dramatic difference between SCC members and the rest of the white

Catholic population is in Mass attendance. Two out of three SCC members attend Mass at least once a week, while only 13 percent seldom or never attend Mass. That contrasts with the 31 percent of the general population who attend weekly, and 57 percent that seldom/never attends Mass. In the 2000 publication, 93 percent of SCCs attended Mass at least once a week. And it is not surprising then that our Level of Commitment Index, based on Mass attendance, how important they say the Church is to them, and whether they might leave the Church, shows only 3 percent with a low commitment, compared to 17 percent among the general population, and at the other end more than 4 in 10 SCC members compared with one in six of the general population having a high commitment to the Church.

Table 1.2 compares SCCs with the general population on aspects of being Catholic that are very important to them.

Table 1.2: Percentages of SCC members and rest of White Population saying aspects of church teachings are Very important to them

	SCCs	Population
Helping the poor is	77%	61%
Working for social justice	59	25
Church teachings opposing the death penalty	44	17
Church teachings opposing same-sex marriage	56	29
Church teachings opposing abortion	70	31
Having a daily prayer life	76	38

There are significant differences on all items, with helping the poor and working for social justice, as well as having a daily prayer life especially hopeful signs. While only 44 percent say Church teaching opposing the death penalty is very important to them, that is more than twice as many as among the general population. More than 7 in 10 say the Church's opposition to abortion is very important to them, as do 56 percent regarding the Church's opposition to same-sex marriage. They are indeed different from the general population in these matters.

Table 1.3 was created to get some idea of how closely Catholics supported the Church's teachings on social justice and military expenditures, based on the U.S. bishops' peace and economy pastorals of the 1980s.

Table 1.3 Percentages of SCCs and rest of white population who agree strongly or somewhat

	SCCs	Population
More government funds for health care for Poor children	72%	77%
More government funds for the military	59	56
Stiffer Enforcement of the death penalty	54	59
Reduce spending on nuclear weapons	74	81
Further cutbacks in welfare programs	48	48

On these five items they do not differ from the general population. They do support more government funds for health care for poor children, and by a small majority they oppose more cutbacks in welfare programs. Three out of four also support reduced spending on nuclear weapons.

Table 1.4 provides a window into an area of their life that indirectly at least separates them from the rest of the Catholic population—namely active participation in the Mass and parish life.

Table 1.4: Percentages of SCC, National Population, and SCCs in Catholic Experience of Small Christian Communities who were/are active in various church roles

	SCC	Pop.	Catholic Exp.
a. Reader at Mass	38%	14%	32%
b. Eucharistic minister	37	6	44
c. Greeter/usher	39	14	26
d. Altar server	37	16	
e. Music ministry	39	9	
f. Parish committee member	49	12	
g. Are/was member of RENEW	36	3	52
h. Registered member of parish	93	60	81

In all items, SCC members are significantly more active than are other Catholics. At least one in three SCC members are or have been active in such roles as Eucharistic minister, lector, altar server, music ministry, and usher. This is more than two and even three times that of the general white Catholic population. Almost half of SCC members are or have been members of parish committees. And more than nine in ten are registered members in a parish, compared with six in ten of the other Catholics.

Table 1.5 touches on two areas I find interesting, although perhaps not central to membership in SCCs, namely, where they are regarding being religious and spiritual, and other beliefs.

Table 1.5: Percentage of SCC members and white Catholic population who say they are:

	SCC	Population
Religious and spiritual	82%	42%
Religious but not spiritual	4	15
Spiritual but not Religious	9	33
Not religious and not spiritual	4	11

They believe in:

	SCC	Population
Reincarnation	25%	30%
Spiritual energy in trees, rocks, etc.	39	38
Yoga, as a spiritual practice	40	26
Real Presence of Jesus in Eucharist	90	56

Most telling, they are twice as likely as other Catholics (82% to 42%) to say that they are both religious and spiritual, with only one in ten saying they were spiritual but not religious, compared with one in three of other Catholics.

Finally, nine in ten believe in the real presence of Jesus in the Eucharist, which is true of only 56 percent of other Catholics. 40 percent say yoga is a spiritual practice.

In summary, SCC Catholics are more likely to have had a Catholic school/college education than other white Catholics, to be older, to be registered in a parish, to be married to a Catholic, to have that marriage recognized by the Church, to be at Mass at least once a week, and to be highly committed to the Church. They are also more likely to be supportive of the Church's teachings on social justice and peace. They are much more involved in parish life, taking an active role in the liturgy, and in serving on parish committees. They declare themselves to be religious and spiritual, with minorities also declaring belief in reincarnation, yoga and finding spiritual energy in rocks, trees, and other parts of nature. And nine in ten believe in the real presence. For sure, they are gathered. To the extent that active participation in Church and parish life may be a sign of being also sent, there is evidence of that.

In concluding I return to the quotation taken from the writing of Robert K. Merton, about the narratives that constitute the stories of our lives, and of the reference groups and significant others who help shape the character of our thought and inquiry. How it is that our intellectual development is affected by the micro as well as macro environments in which we have lived, and how our story in the end is so much affected by the historical moment at which we entered our particular field.

As I read the draft chapters from and interacted with the other colleagues who contributed to this volume, I came to appreciate the many ways in which Bernard Lee had become a significant other in their lives, too, and how the particular times and events during which we have interacted with and learned from Bernard as well as from each other have so influenced and continue to influence the micro and macro environments in which we all live. By now it must be obvious how much Bernard has influenced my life and research interests, as reflected in all that I have written above. The experience of working with a practical theologian who appreciated what the social sciences have to offer, would have been reward enough. By urging me to ask questions about the meaning of spirituality in the lives of the people we were studying, he provided me an opportunity to recognize my own efforts to be spiritual as well as religious, and to recognize how they have interacted in my own life. For that, and the opportunity to meet and share time with my fellow authors, I am forever grateful.

References

Adversity.Net/education_2_carolina.htm

Camille, Michael. 1992. *Imagination Edge: The Margins in Medieval Art*. Cambridge, MA: Harvard University Press.

Cowan, M. and Lee, B. 1997. *Conversation, Risk & Conversion: The Inner and Public Life of Small Christian Communities*. Maryknoll, NY: Orbis Books, 1997.

D'Antonio, William V., Michele Dillon, and Mary L. Gautier. 2013. *American Catholics in Transition*. Lanham, MD: Rowman and Littlefield Publishers

Lee, Bernard. 2000. *Habits for the Journey: A Mystical and Political Spirituality for Small Christian Communities*. Dayton: North American Center for Marianist Studies.

Lee, Bernard, with William V. D'Antonio et al. 2000. *The Catholic Experience of Small Christian*

Communities. Mahwah, NJ: Paulist Press.

Merton, Robert K. 1987. pp 19-20, In *Sociological Lives: Social Change and the Life Course,*

Volume 2. Matilda Riley (ed.).Newbury Park, CA: Sage Publications.

Moore, Gerard, SM. 2002, March. "A Spirituality for Justice," *Catholic Social Justice Series*. North

Sydney, NSW: The Australian Catholic Social Justice Council.

1   Lee, B. *The Catholic Experience of Small Christian Communities.*
2   Camille, Michael. *Image on the Edge: The Margins in Medieval Art.* (Cambridge: Harvard University Press, 1992).
3   Cowan and Lee, 1997, 11.
4   Moore, G. March 2002, 5
5   Riley, Matilda (ed), *Sociological Lives*, 1987, pp 19-20.
6   D'Antonio, William V., Michele Dillon, and Mary L. Gautier. 2013. *American Catholics in Transition*. Lanham, MD: Rowman and Littlefield Publishers

Chapter 11

Living Religiously in the 21ˢᵗ Century

Bernard J. Lee, S.M.

Linking Three Themes

My reflections will be around three themes.

I will first borrow from cultural anthropology to distinguish between "deep story" and "charism," which is a pragmatically useful distinction—not just intellectually but functionally. (Or so I hope!)

Second, I propose to look at some changes in Religious Life since Vatican II for critical insight and (perhaps) guidance for post-Conciliar religious life. The collaboration between religious communities and lay women and men I believe to be critical. But! – that means laywomen and laymen profoundly formed in the religious community's deep story, who have become real participants in it and contributors to new interpretations and understandings of it. Third and last, I will focus upon some cultural contextualization of contemporary young adults, and look for some clues to our religious-life futures as ready interactors with these young people. Six or eight significant books concerning young adults have come out in the last ten or twelve years. A widespread effort to understand and interpret these young adults is a good clue that something significant is going on here.

I. Deep story and charism

I am indebted to Peter Worsley's book on cultural anthropology, *The Trumpet Shall Sound,* and to Stephen Crites' article, "The Narrative Quality of Experience," for the reflections that follow.[1] I will be using words more fitted to conversation about religious life than theirs which are drawn more from cultural anthropology.

Principally, I will take the word "charism" that we frequently use about our communities, and break it into two separate notions: "Deep Story" and "Charism," which I believe offer some guidance to us. The ways that social scientists describe a charismatic person has some pay-off in understanding charism in religious life. Deep Story is our narrative character—the story-line—which connects us from era to era to era. Our deep stories, our narrative structures, give us our continuity over time. I do not believe that charism can be transmitted into a different era, recovered as it were. It can only be reconstituted, reinvented, and will not ever be identical to its predecessors.

First, Deep Story

Every culture has what I will call a Deep Story, a narrative structure. It gets modified and transformed in different eras, without giving up its basic narrative structure. When we read our respective histories, we understand the non-negotiable pieces that keep showing up. Some words and ideas change—but there is something always steadily identifiable—that is what I am calling a community's Deep Story.

No one can ever exhaustively tell their Deep Story. You can catch the American Deep Story if you read Lincoln's speeches, see "Gone with the Wind," listen to Johnny Cash and Joan Baez, stroll down Broadway in New York, visit the Cathedral of the Immaculate Conception in Washington, D.C.

No one can ever tell a Deep Story, but what we can do is cite instances that reflect it, none of which exhausts it. Deep Stories can vary and develop without losing their identifiable character. The ways a *Rule of Life* gets reinterpreted and restated and revised by General Chapters is an example of change that also stays the same.

Deep Stories are clear to our experience, even as they evade any complete telling of them, and they will even be differently shaped, but still identifiable, from one nation's culture to the next.

Now, Charism

When in popular usage we say that someone or some group has "charisma" we are really naming their perceived effectiveness in the world in which we and he or she lives—effectiveness perhaps with flair. Not just a bit effective in passing, but hugely engaging, publicly appreciated. Charism names a very highly effective connection between a deep story and a contemporary social situation, and it is an effective connection that is widely perceived and named and praised.

But here's the catch: Charism is never a claim one makes for oneself. It is a public perception of the profound effectiveness of a group, normally at work in a difficult and challenging time. Charism does not appear in settled times. And today, I believe, is indeed not a settled time! Charism names a public perception of something experienced as extraordinary. President Kennedy could not have made himself a charismatic presence; others decided that. The public experience of some community that a way of living is both faithful to its deep story and provocatively and effectively responsive to the cry of the age is what is essential to what I am trying to identify as charism.

The following paraphrase of Worsley's description of what is going on when a charismatic person emerges applies usefully, I believe, to religious orders. First, something is happening in a culture in which a number of people have possibly utopian or unrealized aspirations. I sense that this is now a time open to both civil and religious charism. Second, there is someone or some group able to articulate those poignant aspirations, and consolidate them because he or she (or a small group) embodies these values and aspirations, and knows them from the inside out. Third, what such a person or group needs to do, finally, is to "become the basis of collective social action, and to be perceived, invested with meaning, and acted upon by significant others.[2] There is some avid following! Fourth, no one is ever "charismatic" alone, on one's own. A person or a group has to be publicly recognized, socially validated, and able to attract followers. But it would be folks out there, beyond the insider group, that judge charisma to be at work (doesn't have to be that word). And that is when followers start happening, joiners, people hooking their destiny to what the world apparently feels is needed. A religious order begins and/or continues when people are hooking their destiny to charisma palpably at work.

These sociological indicators help us understand how charism can and does happen with religious orders. But I would say the same thing about Roman Catholicism. People know when it has gone to work very, very effectively either within the Church's life, or within the Church's impact on wider culture. But it's in wider culture that the acknowledgement of charism occurs—it is never a self-description—or at least should never be attempted as self-description.

I think it fair to say that charism is always part of the initiation of a new religious community. A new deep story is initiated at a charism-potential moment. The deep story can continue. But charism will have to be reinvented over and over, and never as self-conferral—but when the Deep Story is once again profoundly and effectively at work in the world, and is recognized and validated by others, not by the community, at least, not by us alone.

Our Church and our world are ripe for Deep Stories capable of charism, to which disciplined high imagination is critical. The other word for that is "prophetic imagination": Knowing how to live now in view of the world that needs to come into existence.

It's my guess that ecclesial culture is ripe for having its Deep Story modified and recast, especially with reference to our younger generation. The polarization of both religious and civic culture cries out for courage and vivid imagination—both of which appear more readily in young hearts, but need the support of our older hearts.

I find it instructive as well as intriguing that while Greeks center personhood in the head, Hebrews center it in the heart. I was born a Greek Catholic but somewhere along the line turned into a Hebrew Catholic! Heart indeed needs head. But heart is where the aching excitement occurs that can stir a world.

I conclude this section with an ascetical challenge—at least it is a large one for me. If as a community we are not imaginatively, effectively, and pastorally, i.e., charismatically, speaking to our age, our survival chances are limited. That frightens me, because I want my community to last. And that is the wrong reason. I must give myself heart and soul to this challenge because I believe that we have something to give that the reign of God in the world desperately needs. It's for God's sake that we respond with power and imagination, not for us to survive. I think of Becket's remark in T. S. Eliot's play *Murder in the Cathedral,* when the devil tempts him to suffer martyrdom so that he can look down from heaven on his killers in hell. And Thomas says, "The last temptation is the greatest treason, to do the right deed for the wrong reason." The right reason is offering what we can to what the world needs, for God's sake!

There is part of a poem in Naomi Shihab Nye's book of poetry, *Yellow Glove,* that catches the spirit of the difference between charism and deep story:

TELLING THE STORY

Some start out
with a big story
that shrinks.
Some stories accumulate power
like a sky gathering clouds, quietly, quietly
till the story rains around you.
Some get tired of the same story
and quit speaking.
What will we learn today?
There should be an answer,
and it should
change.[3]

II. Second Vatican Council and after

I will risk an historical assessment here—or maybe just a guess.

The late 1940s until the early 1960s were an unusual time for religious orders in this country. Following World War II, he numbers of new members was unnaturally high, partly because Catholic identity was quite clear and compelling. Religious life had for a long while been called the life of perfection. But Vatican II made it clear that all people are called to the same perfection. That leveled the playing field! The exodus from religious life was huge. My Province's sixty-person formation Center at St. Mary's University had become too small, so we built a facility in the mid-1960s with two hundred rooms. Well, you know the story!

Sometime around 1970 I was interacting with some fellow Brothers before we entered the auditorium to hear a presentation by a renowned speaker. My colleague said to me, "If I hear one more person says that this is a time of profound change, I think I'll throw up." He didn't throw up, but that was the opening sentence. Times of great ecclesial changes leave their mark on lay, religious, and clerical life. The departures of many religious I would guess is somewhat connected to Vatican II's recognition that "the family is a kind of school of deeper humanity."[4]

So here is one guess I am making. With the decline in numbers of members of religious orders and the increase of respect for the lay apostolic calling, I surmise that religious orders who connect effectively with lay people who share, and perhaps even co-own its Deep Story, stand the best chance of making charism happen once again. The co-ownership is often felt to be risky by religious communities. Real co-ownership means sharing power, sharing in decision making, not just "collaborating with." Our point is not to make charism happen. No one can control that or organize that. Our point is to reorganize how we give our Deep Story a chance to take off in a new way—a way that is radically responsive to what appears actually to be the case in the contemporary Church.

At an annual gathering of the College Theology Society at St. Mary's in San Antonio, I attended a presentation by Professor Rose Beal from St. Mary's in Minnesota. Her topic was "A Lesson from Lasallean Christian Brothers for Lay Theologians Today." She said that "De la Salle had to demonstrate that it was preferable that the Brothers remain laymen in order better to serve the church and participate in its mission. In the mid-twentieth century, Congar and Sauvage had to make bold claims concerning the apostolic character of the whole church, the active role of the laity in the church and its mission, and the potential for spiritual competence on the part of the laity."

Most of us have welcomed lay partners along the way—people who collaborate with us. What I am suggesting is religious and lay collaboration on a different but equal basis: genuine co-ownership of the Marianist or Franciscan or Dominican or Mercy or Jesuit or La Sallean deep story. This would require profound collaborative instincts, and perhaps (even probably!) many new organizational transformations, especially of formational dynamics. I certainly do not have any concrete directions. A lot of us are struggling to find a model that feels like it's the collaboration of equals—not just others joining our mission.

I think some of us in religious life have been building in that direction, which calls for a wider ownership of our Deep Story and shared stewardship of it. To quote Shakespeare: "Tis a consummation devoutly to be wished." At least it is for me! A possible direction with hope as its name. At least, maybe so!

For all religious communities, I suspect the transformations will reflect collaboration with lay women and men on an equal basis, not to survive, but because this is possibly a new collaborative arrangement in Ecclesia. Not third order membership, but some form of real membership with a voice. This is technically, canonically and organizationally challenging.

I say that knowing the challenge that it is to my community as well. There were Lay Marianist men and women in Bordeaux for sixteen years before the Marianist Sisters came into existence in 1816, and the Brothers of Mary (male Marianists) in 1817. The three branches are autonomous but interdependent. We are struggling also to put collaboration on an equal basis.

Now we turn attention to the culture young adults in Western culture. They are a new kind of young culture – one with different consequences than we have addressed in any past history. They are a lovely group and also an independent group – but also a dialogic group if they know their voice matters.

III. Young adults in Western culture

As an "old adult" trying to reflect upon "young adults," I am conscious of words of T.S. Eliot from *Burnt Norton* in *The Four Quartets*:

> Words strain,
> Crack and sometimes break, under the burden,
> Decay with imprecision, will not stay in place,
> Will not stay still.

It was Andrew Greeley who in the '60s coined the phrase "the new breed" about young adults. I sense that what they are today is in continuity with the profound changes that began in the '60s—those were just the beginning stages, but already identifiable. I was a student in Berkeley in the late 60s and early 70s, and watched some of the new becoming of young adults from up close.

The phrase "young adults" gets defined in multiple ways. I have in mind late teens, and then through the twenties and into the thirties. There are about 50,000,000 such young adults in the United States, about a fourth of whom, some 12,500,000, identify as Catholic. But only some 16-20% of them (different studies vary a bit but are close to this) regularly participate in the life of the Church. But the other 80% of them still identify as Catholic. They are not hostile; they are just not actively connected.

The following quotations are from scattered places throughout the book *Young Adult Catholics* by Dean Hoge, et al. They certainly ring true to my experience of young adults. I don't cite them because I know the right response to them – but perhaps so that we can share wisdom and inventiveness. These all ring true to me.

> Most young adult Catholics are not angry at the church. They are simply distanced from it. In spite of this weaker institutional connection, the majority of young Catholics "like being Catholic," and can't imagine themselves being anything other than Catholic.
>
> Significant numbers of young adult Catholics today no longer see the Roman Catholic Church as unique or essential, the pope as necessary, the Church's structures as important or tradition as a source of objective truth . . . This is not exclusively a failure of leadership. It is part of the larger alienation of all authoritative institutions that is taking place in all American religious communities.
>
> Many young adults have a difficult time articulating a coherent sense of Catholic identity.
>
> While young adult Catholics rank social justice high in what they regard as essential to their faith, the relationship between social justice and a specific Catholic identity remains unclear . . . If the relationship between social justice and a specifically Catholic identity were more immediate to young adult Catholics, their perspective might be more concerned with structural approaches, aggregate effects, power, and institutional systems – in keeping with contemporary Church teachings regarding social justice.

On the positive side, this shift toward individual religious identity-construction allows a greater assumption of responsibility within the tradition by many young adult Catholics for their religious and spiritual life—as mandated by Vatican II. Unlike their evangelical counterparts, the current generation of young adult Catholics is less theologically orthodox than their elders. Many young adult Catholics complained of the absence of meaningful young adult ministries and activities in their parishes.

Aside from activities associated with involvement with church, social justice initiatives, and intermittent use of the sacraments, it is not clear what, behaviorally speaking, constitutes commitment to the mission of the Church among many young adults. Institutional Catholicism is simply not of central importance in their lives. The type of positive approach associated with the Rite of Christian Initiation of Adults (RCIA) with its emphasis on mentoring, deliberation, community, and discipleship, is a helpful model. People who experience empowerment through the church will become stronger Catholics.

The communal nature of the Church should be emphasized. More attention and energy should be given to building community in parish life. But the liturgy alone should not bear the entire burden of this task. Small faith communities and action-oriented projects will also be important. This community building initiative should not be construed simply as bringing back young adults who are feeling isolated and in need of support and intimacy. Young adults must see that community is an ecclesial dimension that is intrinsic to their Catholic identity and God, or even between the individual and the hierarchy representing God; they must feel that it is a community-mediated and community-articulated identity.

This is where having institutional collaborators, parents and young adults as co-owners of any religious order's deep story could be hugely and insightfully energizing. Each group would do it differently. I certainly do not know absolutely for sure that a new lay-religious co-ownership of Deep Story is the way to go. But I believe it to be worth seriously entertaining as a possibility. That would perhaps mean giving lay members voting rights and some form of participation in leadership structures and Chapters. Mostly, it will take imagination, not just suggestions but some wild guesses, some eschatological hope, that "something else might be the case!"

If one tries to situate religious life in the contemporary Church, the avenues of approach are manifold. I have used three of them: (1) the important distinction between a community's Deep Story and its potential to become effectively charismatic; (2) Vatican II and perfection as everyone's calling – a new framework for collaboration between lay and religious; and (3) the critical call in religious communities to take seriously the social matrix of todays' young adults. All three of these belong together. They are of a piece. This is not the only way to assess the contemporary context for religious life, but perhaps it does suggest some avenues for active religious communities.

A closing surmise

I now recall a "sort of admonition" from my Church history Professor, the renowned Dominican church historian, Marie-Humbert Vicaire, at the Universite de Fribourg in Switzerland where I did seminary. It was the 1964-65 academic year, while the Second Vatican Council was in session, and hopes and excitement were sky high. In the midst of the exhilaration, Pere Vicaire sounded a note of caution.

Most church councils and diocesan synods were called to address troubled times or greatly disputed issues. Only relatively few, he said, were called for up-dating, for deliberately and seriously moving forward. These councils, Pere Vicaire observed, created huge initial, responsive excitement. But then, fear took hold as the changes took shape, and there were long periods of retrenchment. Only when the Church finally worked those reactions out of its system could the reforms really get underway. Sometimes for such councils and/or synods, one must wait until the new batch of leaders are not old enough to remember a "before the Council" period—that would be perhaps bishops and theologians ages 45-60.

The excitement after Vatican II is still vivid for those of us old enough to remember the before and after. Mass was in Latin. Eucharist is now in English. Sometimes the closing music at Eucharistic Liturgy was "Le the Sun Shine In," from the raucous musical, "Hair." Adults sang them too—and certainly young adults. There was Ray Repp's music, and then the St. Louis Jesuits.

But soon in the 90s and beyond, there were pull-backs and hesitations. We know the story. I then remembered Pere Vicaire's comments from 25 years earlier. The previous Pope often celebrated the Eucharist in Latin, sometimes pictured with his back to the gathered community

Now I am not yet sanguinely optimistic, but hopeful that that new era might be imminent. There are some interesting recent movements. A significant number of priests in Austria have formed a new organization with members from both diocesan clergy and religious orders, pushing for some major reforms in both theology and practice, such as the ordination of married men. There is a similar organization in Germany, with some noted theologians among the members, also in Australia, the United States, and Ireland.

The Vatican investigation of American religious women is stirring wide interest, as well as considerable out-loud wide support for these remarkable women. Seven Provinces of Franciscan Friars, the Cincinnati Province of the Missionaries of the Precious Blood, and the international head office of the Xaverian Brothers have passed resolutions of support for LCWR. At its recent meeting in St. Louis in early June, the Catholic Theological Society passed a resolution in support of religious women in this country.

One of the pieces of wisdom that I have taken from process theology, especially from the writings of Bernard Loomer, is the difference between unilateral power and relational power. One never tries to exert influence in any group by which one has not first been affected.

The 12,500,000 young adult Catholics in this country are an interesting group. They identify as Catholic, even though only 16-20% of them are regularly active. But they still claim Catholic identity! I have a lot of them in my classes at St. Mary's University. I wonder whether they are waiting, and if so, what they are waiting for.

So I wonder, I really wonder, if perhaps the reaction to Vatican II is out of our system, or getting there with some last blasts, and whether the Second Vatican Council is perhaps about to happen. I know that sounds dramatic, but it's worth pondering at least momentarily. Maybe we have worked some resistances out of our system. My interaction with young adults suggests that it's a possibility worth pondering. I do not know whether this is a reasonable idea to entertain, or just – once more – "a consummation devoutly to be wished."

Young adults: Some helpful resources

D'Antonio, William; Davidson, James; Hoge; Dean; and Wallace, Ruth. *Laity: American and Catholic / Transforming the Church.* Sheed & Ward.

William D'Antonio; Davidson, James; Hoge, Dean; and Gautier, Mary. *American Catholics Today: New Realities of Their Faith and Their Church.* Sheed & Ward.

D'Antonio, William, Anthony Pogorelc, *et al. Voices of the Faithful: Loyal Catholics Striving for Change.* New York: 2007.Crossroad, Herder & Herder:

Hoge, Dean; Dinges, Johnson, William, Mary; and Gonzales, Juan. *Young Adult Catholics: Religion in the Culture of Choice.* University of Notre Dame Press.

Pearce, Lisa; and Denton, Melinda Lundquist. *A Faith of Their Own: Stability and Change in the Religiosity of America's Adolescents.* Oxford University Press

Smith, Christian, with Patricia Snell. *Souls in Transition: The Religious & Spiritual Lives of Emerging Adults.* New York: Oxford University Press.

Wuthnow, Robert. *After the Baby Boomers: How Twenty- and Thirty-Somethings are Shaping the Future of American Religion.* Princeton University Press.

Wuthnow, Robert. *Sharing the Journey: Support Groups and America's New Quest for Community.* Macmillan Free *Press.*

---

1   Peter Worsley, The Trumpet Shall Sound. NY: Schocken, 1968; Stephen Crites, "The Narrative Quality of Experience." *Journal of the American Academy of Religion* (39), 1971.
2   Worsley, op.cit., 16.
3   Naomi Shihab Nye, "Telling the Story," in *Yellow Glove.* 1986.
4   Gaudium et Spes, #52.

TRUE DIRECTIONS

An affiliate of Tarcher Books

OUR MISSION

Tarcher's mission has always been to publish books
that contain great ideas. Why? Because:

GREAT LIVES BEGIN WITH GREAT IDEAS

At Tarcher, we recognize that many talented authors, speakers,
educators, and thought-leaders share this mission and deserve to be
published – many more than Tarcher can reasonably publish ourselves.
True Directions is ideal for authors and books that increase awareness,
raise consciousness, and inspire others to live their ideals and passions.

Like Tarcher, True Directions books are designed to do three things:
inspire, inform, and motivate.

Thus, True Directions is an ideal way for these important voices to
bring their messages of hope, healing, and help to the world.

Every book published by True Directions– whether it is non-fiction, memoir,
novel, poetry or children's book – continues Tarcher's mission to publish works
that bring positive change in the world. We invite you to join our mission.

For more information, see the True Directions website:
www.iUniverse.com/TrueDirections/SignUp

Be a part of Tarcher's community to bring positive change in this world!
See exclusive author videos, discover new and exciting books, learn about
upcoming events, connect with author blogs and websites, and more!
www.tarcherbooks.com

TRUE DIRECTIONS
AN AFFILIATE OF TARCHER BOOKS

Printed in the United States
By Bookmasters